Mexican Americans in Texas
A Brief History

Arthur S. Link
General Editor for History

Mexican Americans in Texas

A BRIEF HISTORY

Arnoldo De León
Angelo State University

HARLAN DAVIDSON, INC.
ARLINGTON HEIGHTS, ILLINOIS 60004

Library of Congress Cataloging-in-Publication Data

De León, Arnoldo, 1945–
    Mexican Americans in Texas: a brief history / Arnoldo
    De León
        p.   cm.
    Includes index.
    ISBN 0-88295-902-6
    1. Mexican Americans—Texas—History.
    2. Texas—History.
I. Title.
F395.M5D37   1993
976.4'0046872—dc20   92-29819
                                                   CIP

Cover design: DePinto Graphic Design

Manufactured in the United States of America
97 96 95 94 93 1 2 3 4 5 MG

Contents

Contents

Preface

SERIOUS scholarly study of Mexican Americans in Texas goes back only to the early 1970s. It is true that historians before that decade wrote on the Spanish colonial era (circa 1519 to 1821) and even touched on some aspects of Texas-Mexican life during Mexico's rule of the province (1821–1836). But their interests stopped there, for they assumed that Tejano society collapsed when Anglo Texans established an American rule following the 1836 war for Texas independence against Mexico. To be sure, a smattering of theses, dissertations, and academic articles on Mexican Americans did appear before 1970, but by and large, historians mistakenly believed that Tejanos lacked a distinct history worthy of scholarly attention.

Then, in the late 1960s, there appeared in Mexican-American communities throughout the country what is termed the "Chicano Movement," an ethnic-charged explosion of cultural pride that called for fundamental changes in society. Among other things, activists in colleges and high schools throughout different parts of the United States, supported by faculty members, community leaders, parents, journalists, bureaucrats, and others, demanded the dismissal of racist educators, the alteration of a curriculum which they viewed as ethnocentric, the recruitment of more Mexican-American teachers and administrators, and the development of classes in Mexican-American history. Elements of the scholarly community heeded the latter cry by concentrating their research on what came to be known as "Chicano history," a scholarly inquiry that utilized revisionist approaches to meet several objectives:

to wit, determine the origins for Mexican-American subordination throughout the United States, chronicle the Mexican-American participation in the historical process, and, ultimately, attempt the integration of the Mexican-American experience into the United States' saga.[1] Some historians chose to narrow their interests to the history of Mexican people in the state of Texas. Their efforts during the last two decades have yielded a rich harvest of scholarly tomes. This survey is sensitive to that literature.

In writing Chicano history, many scholars followed an unwritten assumption that the history of Mexican-descent people in the United States began when citizens of Mexico became Mexican Americans. The year 1848 would, therefore, be the logical starting point, for it was then that the United States, victorious in the War with Mexico (1846–1848), acquired the modern-day states of California, New Mexico, Arizona, Colorado, and parts of Utah and Nevada. The Treaty of Guadalupe Hidalgo, which ended the war, gave United States citizenship to the Mexican occupants of those territories. In comparison, Mexican residents of Texas had become citizens of the Texas Republic when Anglo Americans acquired their independence from Mexico. Though Mexican people in Texas were not technically United States citizens until 1845, when Texas became a state in the Union, historians recognized 1836 as the year in which they became an ethnic group, since for all intents and purposes, Anglo citizens of the Republic were ideologically and culturally Americans.[2]

Despite this general consensus regarding periodization for Chicano history, I have followed the advice of more recent revisionist writers who argue that Tejano history ought to be stretched back to the colonial era when Spaniards initially penetrated the Texas wilderness. These scholars remind us that Spanish-Mexicans, the first to transplant European civilization to Texas, gave names to numerous places and rivers, contributed to the region's material culture, and were the predecessors of today's Mexican-American citizens of Texas. Spanish-Mexican pioneers carried forth into the American epoch their: cultural accoutrements; institutions; survival mechanisms; sentimental attachment to the land of their birth or upbringing; approach toward land usage; agricultural work rhythms; family and gender relations; and numerous other aspects of community living.

Stressing such continuity, these historians note that Tejano society did not face exhaustion in 1836 but crossed nationhoods without much disruption. This line of analysis seems imperative to correct the pre–1970s scholarship which minimized the historical role of people of Mexican descent by implying that Tejano civilization became inert when American rule supplanted Spanish and Mexican. The first two chapters of this book, thus, attempt to bridge the history of Spaniards and Mexicans who lived in the land that became modern-day Texas prior to 1836 and that of Mexican Americans who maintained residence in the state as Americans citizens after that year.[3]

During the last twenty years of revisionism, due in part to the Chicano Movement, historians have written Tejano history from approaches that stress the mistreatment of Mexican Americans, the Tejano resistance to victimization, but also the adjustments Mexican Americans have made in order to meld with the mainstream United States society. In these pages, I employ those themes but my purpose is also to emphasize the process of cultural syncretization, the presence of class variations within the minority population itself, and the diversity that separates Tejanos residing in the diverse geographic regions of the state. I am particularly interested in portraying Texas Mexicans as subjects in the ongoing Texas story and not merely as objects being acted upon.

In writing this book, I have also tried to keep a particular student audience in mind. *Mexican Americans in Texas* may be used as a core text for classes that deal specifically with the history of Mexican Americans in Texas (Tejanos) or as a useful supplement to courses in Mexican-American, Texas, and American history.

Throughout the book, I use different definitions to identify Spanish-Mexican descent people. The term "Tejano" refers to those of Mexican origin, regardless of nativity, who resided, or reside, within the modern boundaries of Texas from the early eighteenth century to the present. I utilize the term "Texas Mexican" in writing about Mexican-descent people after 1821, for it was at that time when Texas ceased being a part of the Spanish empire and its settlers became citizens of a new sovereignty, namely the newly independent country of Mexico. Though the government of the Republic of Texas gave Tejanos a new citizenship after 1836, their own designation remained "Mexican," and in any event, Anglo Americans called them by that name, albeit disparagingly. "Texas Mexican," therefore, seems appropriate for usage after Chapter Two. I apply the ascription "Mexicans" broadly, also for the period after 1821, to include both native and foreign born Mexican-origin inhabitants of the state. I employ the label "Mexican American" synonymously with the above terminology, but only in discussing the period after 1845. In that year, people of Mexican ancestry in what is Texas today became citizens of the United States. "Mexican Americans" implies United States citizenry, whether by birth or naturalization. The term "Chicano" was not used in public discourse until the 1960s, so it is not found until Chapter Nine, where it is placed in proper historical context: in that era the word came to symbolize a particular political ideology and a cultural emphasis on Mexico's heritage, including its pre-Columbian past. I reserve the title "Hispanic" for the post–1976 era, when it became part of the popular lexicon, again to identify individuals of Spanish-Mexican descent. Folks who migrate from Mexico are referred to as "immigrants."

I owe a debt of gratitude to numerous scholars who made suggestions for revisions of my original manuscript, but the remarks of three readers were especially helpful. My special thanks go to Jesús F. de la Teja of Southwest Texas State University, Richard Griswold del Castillo of San Diego State University, and Emilio Zamora, Jr., of the University of Houston. Dr. Zamora's insightful commentary proved particularly valuable and led me to rethink some of the book's earlier themes.

CHAPTER ONE

Texas: A Spanish Outpost
1716–1790s

MEXICAN AMERICANS in Texas descend from people whose ancestry is Spanish and Mexican Indian. After the Spanish conquest of present-day Mexico in the early sixteenth century, Iberian males intermixed with Indian women. Cultures also blended, and those people of a blended heritage and culture moved northward from Mexico and laid the foundation for what would become Mexican-American communities in the United States. Since that time to this day, immigrants to Texas from Mexico continue to bring aspects of a common past with them. The history of Mexican Americans, then, may be traced to the Iberian peninsula.

Iberian and Indian Roots

People from Spain themselves owe their heritage to several civilizations. Like other Europeans, Spaniards became indebted to the Greeks, borrowing much concerning laws and traditions. Rome contributed extensively to Spanish life as well, imposing on Iberia its political institutions, language, and religion. Germanic groups, namely the Visigoths, dominated Spain during the period from the fifth to the eighth centuries, but they ended up fusing their own way of life with that of the cultures they vanquished. When the Moslems conquered Spain around A.D. 711, they preserved native customs and institutions but implanted the best traditions of their native North African civilization.[1]

The Moslem conquest opened a new chapter in Spanish history. During the next seven centuries, the Spaniards waged a war to repel the Moorish invaders and regain control of their nation—this campaign is called the *reconquista*. Not until the year 1492 did the king's *conquistadores* (conquerors) overwhelm the last of the Moors and succeed in extricating them from their last defense lines. With matters at home finally settled, the powerful Spanish Crown was eager to explore the known world in hopes of increasing its wealth. Coincidentally, one Christopher Columbus, sailing under the flag of Spain, departed from Europe in a westerly course with the objective of finding a shorter route to the Indies. Instead, he unexpectedly encountered a new world with new peoples when he landed in the islands now known as the Bahamas on October 12, 1492.

The Madrid government now took up the task of assembling an empire by subduing the "New World" peoples and their lands. Leading the advance into the mainlands of modern-day Latin America were conquistadores whose mission resembled that of those who had regained the Iberian peninsula from the Moslems. One such conquistador, Hernán Cortés, directed the attempt in 1519 to establish Spanish domination of present-day Mexico. As his armed entourage marched from the coast towards the interior, it encountered resistance from indigenous tribes but defeated them with superior European weapons. Convinced that Cortés's apparent invincibility on the battlefield marked the Spaniard as Quetzalcoatl, the legendary god who was prophesied to return from the eastern seas to reclaim his lost lands, the Aztec emperor Montezuma dispatched envoys to show the foreigners into the capital city of Tenochtitlán, located on an island in Lake Texcoco. At Tenochtitlán (today's Mexico City), the Aztecs presented the Spaniards with gold, slaves, and other presents. After a time, however, the foreigners wore out their welcome. In June of 1520, the Aztecs massed to evict the invaders. The Spaniards attempted an escape over a causeway, but the Aztecs killed many of the would-be escapees, destroyed more than forty of their horses, and compelled the surviving Spaniards to scuttle their treasure in the bottom of the lake. That evening became known as *la noche triste* (the sad night).

By April of 1521, however, the Europeans were back in Tenochtitlán, this time better prepared to besiege the city. For three months the Aztecs withstood a Spanish quarantine of their city, but finally the invaders took the town block by block. Cuauhtémoc, the nephew of Montezuma, surrendered Tenochtitlán in August 1521, thereby paving the way for the ruthless Spanish domination of the indigenous Indian population of the rest of the lands they conquered.[2]

The Spanish Colonial Era in Texas

EXPLORATION

The Spaniards wanted to find new lands with riches as valuable as those they found in Tenochtitlán. The reports of one Álvar Núñez Cabeza de Vaca whetted their appetites. Cabeza de Vaca and three others had been shipwrecked in 1528 on an island near present-day Galveston and, after six years of coexisting with local Indian tribes, traversed today's southern and western Texas, finally reaching New Spain, as the modern-day country of Mexico was called until the 1810s, in 1536. Upon arriving in Mexico City, the castaway reported tales of great wealth existing in the lands he had crossed.[3]

Hurriedly, the royal government ordered two expeditions into the unexplored lands of the north. In 1540, Francisco Vásquez de Coronado directed one of these probes and, failing to find anything of substance in what would become New Mexico, headed eastwardly into the modern-day Texas Panhandle. The conquistador encountered nothing to substantiate Cabeza de Vaca's contentions, and his expedition retreated to the interior of New Spain without fulfilling its mission of conquering valuable territories.[4] Followup efforts to discover wealth in New Spain's Far North (the region that belonged to Mexico until 1848 and today constitutes the United States Southwest) met similar defeat.

In subsequent decades, the crown pressed beyond the lands of the early conquests, colonizing the lands of New Spain and South America. Not until the early eighteenth century, however, did the Spaniards see fit to permanently settle Texas (though exploration and Catholic proselytizing among the Indians had persisted intermittently). In 1716, in response to French activity along the Texas coast, the government in Mexico City dispatched Domingo Ramón to present-day East Texas. Behind Ramón marched an entourage of some twelve soldiers, a similar number of missionaries, and several families. Ramón's party colonized an area that would later become Nacogdoches. Two years later, Martín de Alarcón also headed northward with instructions to plant a colony that would act as a midway point between outposts in New Spain's interior and the forts and missionary sites in the eastern part of the province. This expedition founded the presidio of San Antonio de Béxar and the mission of San Antonio de Valero along the San Antonio River.[5]

In 1731, fifty-six immigrants from the Canary Islands (most of them of common stock—fishermen, farmers, and ordinary laborers) arrived on the site, founding a community they named San Fernando de Béxar. Other efforts to protect the coast and Christianize surrounding indigenous tribes explain the origins of La Bahía (Goliad) in 1721. In 1749, officials relocated the site westward along the San Antonio River in anticipation of the establishment of two civil communities.[6]

Authorities delayed the colonization of the Rio Grande until the 1740s and 1750s but then executed some of the most successful settlement projects in the Far North. That success may be attributed to the commitment and foresight of José de Escandón, who colonized regions on both banks of the Rio Grande, among them Laredo (though the belt of land between the Rio Grande and the Nueces River belonged to the state of Tamaulipas until 1848).[7]

POBLADORES

No more than a few thousand souls inhabited the land north of the Nueces River throughout the colonial era. As of the early 1730s, these *pobladores* (settlers) numbered about 500.[8] A census taken in 1777 counted 3,103 people in the territory. Some 2,060 of these lived in the San Antonio complex of the town proper, one presidio, and five missions, 696 made their home in La Bahía, and 347 resided in Nacogdoches. By the 1780s, some 700 persons inhabited the river community of Laredo; although a number of them earned their livelihood from urban vocations, the majority did so as ranchers or ranch hands.[9] It was the responsibility of all these frontierspeople to hold the province for the crown and ward off foreign interlopers.

In the earliest stages of colonization in Texas, the imperial government had recruited settlers from among those conditioned to frontier living, but eventually settlement depended on a voluntary migration. Though movement northward never intensified, people arrived in Texas from New Spain villages in the colonial provinces of Coahuila and

Texas in the
Eighteenth Century

| 0 miles | 100 | 200 |
| 0 km | 100 | 200 |

Nuevo León, others from places as far away as central New Spain.[10] A variety of forces urged migrants to head towards the frontier. Oppressive conditions on the *haciendas* (large rural estates owned by Spanish families and worked by laborers bound to the institution by debt peonage) or in colonial towns, for instance, motivated the more intrepid to search out new surroundings. Talk of better working conditions and improved pay in northern mines or ranches also enticed many into braving the trek north towards the unknown. The chance to find legal or extralegal employment on the frontier as a merchant, a peddler of contraband goods, or even as an outlaw further lured folks away from the land of their upbringing and thrust them into a migratory wave. Natural disasters such as droughts, and severe downturns in New Spain's economy further induced pioneers to strike for the borderlands.[11]

Still, reasons why people from New Spain did not migrate to imperial outposts in great numbers are not difficult to ascertain. Fatal diseases frequently afflicted the population, thereby blunting pressures that ordinarily compel people to relocate. Hacienda owners, facing labor shortages, deterred the mobility of the rural masses, using brute force to prevent the escape of those wanting to flee the grim conditions on the haciendas. Finally, towards the latter decades of the eighteenth century, the crown faced less external threats from foreign competitors and thus pursued a more relaxed colonization policy.[12]

THE FRONTIER ADVANCE

New Spain's advancement towards frontier country may be associated with four well-known institutions. These mainstays of Spanish colonization had their genesis during the reconquista but developed further as New Spain's settlements fanned out towards its northern regions. The crown counted on these institutions to successfully claim and people unsettled territories and to stimulate the pioneer economy. Around them community life converged and cultural life flowered. They gave pobladores a needed feeling of familiarity in a region starkly detached from major centers of population.[13]

The Mission   As a pioneer institution, the mission acted to bring new lands under the king's dominion, expand the empire, civilize new acquisitions, and execute imperial designs. But primarily, it sought to save the Indians' souls and covert them into Catholics and loyal Spanish subjects. Therefore, the sacristans ministered to civilian settlers, government officials, and soldier-settlers by performing a variety of spiritual services, such as keeping religious buildings and administering the sacraments at birth, marriage, and death. Incidentally, mission grounds became magnets for unofficial settlements. Pobladores gravitated towards the compounds which generated economic activity and socialization. From the missionaries all family members learned the Church's beliefs or had them reaffirmed. Missions continued their good work of propagating the Catholic faith until well into the eighteenth century.[14]

The Presidio   The *presidio* had as its function frontier defense. Manned by soldiers trained for conflict with varied hostile elements on the frontier, these garrisons housed soldiers who had the responsibility of laying claim to new territories and guarding those already belonging to the crown, protecting civilians and mission friars from attack by hostile Indians, and policing the missions to insure that the converted Indian neophytes continued their training.[15]

The presidio's presence, furthermore, stimulated demographic and economic growth. Not infrequently, soldiers traveled to their assignments accompanied by their entire families. The institution also enticed local recruits attracted by military pay, privileges, and the uniform. Presidio soldiers often married women from nearby communities, and older soldiers might end their careers in Texas and remain in the territory, further augmenting the size of its population. Finally, the presidios became commercial centers in which farmers sold their agricultural goods, ranchers exchanged livestock products, townfolk conducted mercantile transactions, and tailors, smiths, and other artisans plied their trade.[16]

The Rancho   The Spaniards introduced the *rancho* (ranch) into the borderlands as still another agent of colonization, and though its primary function was to sustain civilian life, over time the institution served a multitude of purposes. First, it helped to safeguard remote sections of the empire from foreign threats. It contributed to the work of the missionaries by producing foods needed to nourish the neophytes. It furnished civil communities with beef, wool, hides, and tallow. It supported the task of the presidios by supplying the soldiers with oxen for plowing, mules for hauling, and horses for mounted troops.[17]

Stock for ranch operations in Texas derived from the abundance of horses, cattle, sheep, and hogs that had been left in Texas by the pre–

eighteenth-century military expeditions (due to unfitness, loss caused by stampedes or accidents, or for the intended purpose of propagation). Expeditions undertaken after the 1710s also brought fresh animals. The earliest stockmen in Texas were actually the missionaries, for the crown had given the Church the first grants of land. Scholarly studies made of the missions in the 1760s find mission lands overrun with semiwild stock. The padres claimed these *mesteños* (ownerless stock) as their own, but settlers encroached upon the herds in desperate efforts at frontier survival.[18]

During the middle eighteenth century, ranching entered a flourishing era, primarily in Central Texas in the land between the San Antonio and the Guadalupe rivers, considered by the historian Jack Jackson to be the cradle of Texas ranching.[19] In San Antonio, industrious stockmen produced meat, soap, and candles for nearby markets and for the local presidio, made tallow and hides for export, and manufactured protective leather gear for the soldiers from cattle by-products. In the distant Piney Woods of East Texas, landowners raised fine horse stock, especially around the Nacogdoches area. In modern-day South Texas, in the expanse between the Rio Grande and the Nueces River, another pastureland thrived, containing unnumbered heads of cattle, sheep, and horses.[20]

By the 1750s, Tejanos had established commercial relations, although illicit, with French Louisiana to the east and Nuevo León and Coahuila to the south. A good amount of contraband in cattle and horses traded for manufactured goods and tobacco from east of the Sabine River came to be conducted on a regular basis, even as royal decrees discouraged the practice.[21] Additionally, Texas cattlemen drove herds southward below the Rio Grande during the 1770s and 1780s. In yearly excursions to the fairs of the town of Saltillo in Coahuila, the pobladores exchanged their cowhides, dried meat, sheepskins, tallow, and other ranch commodities for goods such as foodstuffs and clothes that were impossible to acquire on the frontier.[22]

The Farms   While the frontierspeople planted some crops, few pursued farming on any large scale. Several reasons explain this. First, the pioneers banked on a ranching future tied to their illicit trade with Louisiana. Secondly, civilian farmers had to compete with the missions and even the presidios for a limited buying public. Moreover, farming demanded field hands, but labor was always in short supply on the frontier. Finally, frontierspeople preferred to ranch since livestock could be moved to evade forays by hungry Indians.[23]

Farms, therefore, amounted to little more than hardscrabble ventures. In San Antonio and its environs, townfolk, soldiers and their family members, and Hispanicized Indians did care for small vegetable garden plots using the waters of the San Antonio River and San Pedro Springs for irrigation. In the town of Nacogdoches, frontierspeople raised corn and wheat on residential lots or on surrounding land parcels to satisfy dietary requirements. Since Tejanos found farming neither a simple undertaking nor a profitable enterprise, foodstuff shortages, primarily corn, were common during the eighteenth century.[24]

The Towns   To secure dominion over new lands and defend them, the crown utilized still another frontier institution—the civilian settlement. Four urban sites existed in Texas during the colonial period—Nacogdoches and Goliad were dependent outcroppings of the presidios, missions, and ranches, while San Antonio and Laredo had been founded according to royal ordinances regulating the creation of towns. Within the city space, inhabitants earned their livelihood in various capacities. Some worked as government bureaucrats; craftsmen, including merchants, housebuilders, cobblers, tailors, blacksmiths, and barbers rendered valuable services to the presidios and missions; unskilled workers turned to unspecialized tasks; Hispanicized Indians eked out a living as servants; while an assortment of characters such as jobless migrants or transient peddlers found ways to survive on the urban scene. Others used the urban settlement as a base for commuting to their place of work. These included curates opting for city living, rancheros overseeing their stock operations in absentia, *vaqueros* (cowhands or range hands) working seasonally on the range, and *arrieros* (freighters) transporting foodstuffs, supplies, and building materials between different points in Texas.[25]

In municipalities, pobladores faced conditions not much improved over those in the rural areas. But like their counterparts on the ranchos, city dwellers undertook initiatives to improve their living situations. Communities launched efforts to establish schools, though they frequently confronted difficulties due to unenthusiastic support from the crown. The building of homes amounted to an enormous task considering the settlers' isolation, but they tapped the flora around them, gathering stones, mesquite wood, and coarse grass for *jacales* (huts) and mud (which they mixed with grass) for their *adobes* (mud-walled homes).[26]

Furthermore, the urbanites contended with numerous other adversities. With practically no sewage system on the frontier and water often polluted by litter or carcasses, townspeople had to withstand the threat of diseases (such as small pox and cholera). Health care was often non-existent, as medical personnel preferred the security afforded by the larger cities in the interior of New Spain. Drifters, malcontents, and social misfits who were attracted to the towns added to the permanent residents' daily concerns. Fear of Indian attacks stalked everyone.[27]

FRONTIER COMMUNITY

Isolation, the need for mutual protection, and shared desires to maintain some political independence from the crown forced diverse elements of frontier society to come together to form a community. In time, even the Canary Islanders abandoned their inclination to remain aloof and formed a bond with the rest of the population in Béxar. Ultimately there evolved in Texas a unique frontier identity based on shared circumstances, family ties, and friendships that unified folks from different social strata and racial ancestry, as well as from the ranches, farms, presidios, missions, and towns.[28]

In frontier communities settlers accepted their purpose for being in the Far North, respected royal decrees that they deemed appropriate for maintaining an orderly society, and abided by common-law practices adaptable to the new lands.[29] Culturally, whole communities had common familial arrangements, architecture, foods, religious beliefs, and language. In San Antonio, for example, Bexareños carried on numerous traditions customary to the frontier, several of which were practiced during the month of December. In that month, they celebrated their perseverance in the province by holding festivities, which included the observance of the days of the Immaculate Conception and the Virgin of Guadalupe, as well as bullfights, games, and dances. In between the fall harvest and the spring livestock branding and planting, the tradition of rejoicing in December persisted until the time of the Texas war for independence in 1836.[30] Yet, Tejano culture was not solely the product of the frontier communities; some of the prominent families of Béxar partook in the lifestyle of the prosperous city of Saltillo by vacationing or maintaining houses there, or by sending their children to the schools of that important city.[31]

On the empire's periphery, Tejanos determined their affairs according to immediate needs and concerns. Local interests came before imperial policy, and Tejanos rejected the crown's efforts to dictate demeanor on the frontier.[32] Thus, they defied compliance with rules of civilized behavior as prescribed by the Church and the crown. Instead settlers practiced a conduct designed to elicit excitement from a sometimes dull and dreary life. They organized *fandangos* (festive dancing events) in their own homes wherein those attending took to drinking, carousing, and, from the point of the view of the crown, to unruly comportment. Even though officials frowned disapprovingly upon the sport of horseracing, because organizers generally held them on holy days and observers were inclined to gamble and commit other transgressions, the contests went on. Soldiers themselves violated royal regulations that prohibited their intermingling with the local women; many courted women from nearby civilian settlements, wed them, and began families.[33]

Social Divisions   Colonial Texas society had its social distinctions. Bureaucrats from New Spain's core, presidio officers assigned to the province, rancheros with large herds of livestock, and town merchants selling to the missions, presidios, and ranches, constituted a entrepreneurial sector. As a socioeconomic group, they owned the better homes, worked the more productive ranch lands, and earned the better incomes. They were the ones most creative in developing interstate trade in livestock and goods produced on the frontier. However, they comprised no particular cohort deserving deference or special privileges. In reality, they were no different from the rest of the population in their upbringing, amount of schooling, manner of dress, or racial origin. Their status hinged almost solely on their material accumulations. The above description applies to the standing of the Canary Islanders, who over time relinquished their elite status through biological mixing with the local Bexareños, though some of their descendants did manage to perpetuate a degree of economic comfort.[34]

Underneath the top-level stratum lived the majority of Tejanos, most of them ranch hands, weavers, cobblers, and day laborers. This crust also included some Indian converts who lived marginally in the missions, the presidios, and the ranches. People did not belong to the lower class due to their ethnic background but because of economic misfortune or disadvantage.[35]

Mixed Bloods   Demographers who study the size of Texas's communities in the colonial era note high birth rates but a slow population growth. In remote societies such as those in the Far North, numerous factors inhibited natural reproduction. High death rates among infants, for one, produced a stagnate population. So did the high toll of hazardous frontier living upon the adolescent and adult populations. Furthermore, people on the frontier consumed poor diets and faced recurrent shortages of agricultural products, improper medical attention, and the ever presence of pestilence. The news of Indian attacks in the province discouraged immigration from New Spain's interior, but demographic expansion still resulted principally from in-migration.[36]

Most Tejano pioneers during the colonial era were the product of *mestizaje*, miscegenation among the native Indian populations, European Spaniards, and African slaves. By the seventeenth century, much of New Spain's people were termed *mestizos*, a label applied to the product of unions between Spanish males and Indian women. Though this element comprised the majority population in Texas, various other racial categories existed, including Christianized Indians, mulattoes, and Spaniards. All participated in further racial amalgamation in the province.[37]

Censuses taken in the 1780s actually enumerate more Spaniards than any other classification, but such figures distort actual ancestry. Demographers know that the term "Spanish" did not necessarily identify European, white-skinned Spaniards; instead, it represented a social categorization. In fact, racial makeup could be upgraded on the frontier, as one's racial constitution did not bar upward mobility. Realistically, the term "Spaniard" identified those worthy of a certain status because of accumulated wealth, family connections, military standing, or even distinguished service to the community. European Spaniards, therefore, included but a few government or church appointees. The rest of those labeled Spaniards by the census enumerators were undoubtedly mixed-bloods who "passed" as Spaniards. As noted, the Canary Islanders of San Antonio themselves intermixed with the New Spain–born population, so within two generations following their arrival, no "islander" could claim undiluted blood.[38]

Women on the Frontier   Most pioneer women in the province lived lives similar to those of their counterparts in Tamaulipas, Nuevo León, or Nuevo Mexico. As a group, women in Texas possessed privileges such as the right to judicial redress when necessary and the right to own property whatever their marital status. On the frontier, also, women escaped the more severe proscriptions imposed on them in the heartland, as the hardships of the Far North acted to blur the roles that differentiated the sexes. In Texas, society might also call upon women to perform labor tasks that were traditionally reserved for men and even to physically defend their homes in times of danger.

Nonetheless, male society dictated specific tasks to women, primarily household chores. In the home, wives and mothers had the duty of performing many services for their husbands and families; these included cooking the meals, raising and passing on cultural values to the children, tending the garden plot, making household necessities such as soap, spinning material for cloth, and rendering succor during stressful times.

Furthermore, women lived with slim expectations for improved conditions. Colonial society deemphasized literacy, since reading and writing commanded little value on the frontier. Professional occupations, always limited to a minority of the population, were invariably closed to women. Some aspects of the legal system were also discriminatory. Ending a marriage through divorce, for example, amounted to a major feat, and society tended to ostracize divorcees. As a political bloc, moreover, women mustered little power.[39]

THE LATE EIGHTEENTH CENTURY

Toward the latter decades of the eighteenth century, historical circumstances altered New Spain's relations with the mother country and incidentally the crown's continued domination of Tejanos. First, the Enlightenment's emphasis on equality and the rights of man undermined the thoughts by which the imperial government ruled its possessions throughout Latin America. The example set in 1783 by the North Americans' successful break from England, furthermore, inspired Spain's New World subjects to reconsider colonialism. Finally, in the last decades of the eighteenth century, Spain proved itself inept at dealing with international affairs, embroiling itself in hostilities with France and England. To Latin Americans these costly conflicts seemed senseless. Colonists were pressed with increased taxation and forced donations that helped Spain to finance and prosecute its wars. Widespread resentment within Spain's colonies ensued.[40]

Other events unraveling in Texas further enfeebled the precarious imperial presence in the province. The missions, long fixtures of life on the frontier, declined as centers of Christianization. Enlightenment thinkers back in Spain condemned the Church, the Crown sought to find ways to cut expenditures, threats by foreign powers from east of the Sabine River had dissipated, mission Indians persisted in their dissatisfaction with efforts at their conversion, and Tejano ranchers, coveting the Church's livestock, called upon royal officials to cease government support of the missions. In the 1790s, the government ordered the closing of all Texas missions.[41]

Also by this period, economic fortunes in Texas began slipping. While ranching had gone through cycles of birth and development up to midcentury, it experienced a decline in the 1790s due, ironically, to the excessive numbers of cattle that had been driven to Louisiana and into New Spain's states below the Rio Grande, and to the slaughtering of cattle that roamed public lands. In the face of the downturn, influential families in San Antonio struggling to stay financially sound became even more resentful of royal authority and its taxation decrees.[42]

Throughout most of New Spain, furthermore, job openings and prospects for a better lot decreased during the last years of the colonial period, producing broad discontent among commoners and growing criminality and banditry. In San Antonio, for instance, opportunity for upward mobility lessened during this period.[43]

Political dissatisfaction also heightened. In the last decades of the century, the crown assigned officials to the province of Texas who were more dedicated that their predecessors had been to the serious enforcement of royal decrees, such as those dealing with the cattle industry. Accustomed to a certain amount of autonomy, citizens resisted the new encroachment upon their affairs and protested what they perceived as unjustified close supervision.[44]

CHAPTER TWO

Under Three Nations:
Spain, Mexico, and the Texas Republic
1790s–1836

As Spain's presence in the Far North approached an end in the waning years of the eighteenth century, the core government estimated 5,000 inhabitants living in the region that constitutes Texas today. About one-half of these resided in San Antonio de Béxar and the missions that comprised the town complex. Another 1,200 pobladores made La Bahía their home and approximately 500 lived in Nacogdoches. The river settlement of Laredo (still a part of New Spain's state of Tamauli-pas) was home to some 1,400 people, according to the last census taken by Spanish authorities in 1819.[1]

Identity in the Far North

By this time, the people of Texas and other parts of the Far North prac-ticed a variation of the culture found in New Spain below the Rio Grande. Royal institutions such as the church, the bureaucracy, and the military had not greatly influenced the pobladores. Instead, argues the noted historian David J. Weber, the immediate environment and local circumstances had played more powerful roles in socializing the fron-tierspeople. Remoteness from the center of imperial power had con-ferred upon them a social space, and through time they had developed modes of conduct appropriate to their frontier existence. Given the situation, borderland society was inclined to be more receptive to new thoughts, sentiments, and patterns of living.[2]

Residence in the Far North molded a culture with discernible traits. In the wilderness expanse, the pobladores strove to implant Spanish civilization and protect the region even as the royal government in Mexico City neglected them. This experience, according to Weber and other students of the Far North, fomented a particular regional identity that was a variant of New Spain's culture. Isolation engendered egalitarianism, a sense of duty, and a respect for physical prowess and gallantry in the face of adversity.[3] Those living in Texas accepted a similar ethos, adapting a familiar ranching culture to the new land, enduring the rigors that accompanied life on the range, devising means of wringing a profit from contraband trade (primarily with Louisiana), and taking political stands expressing regional desires. In such a surrounding, there developed an ethic for self-reliance and the feeling that local needs held priority over crown expectations.[4]

By the last years of colonial Texas, several influential families still lived in the province. Concentrated primarily in San Antonio, their concerns also centered less on imperial goals and more on their immediate problems: citizens did not look kindly on soldiers and crown officials who arrived in the early 1800s to reinforce the province against westering citizens from the United States. The new military presence taxed the capacities of the local economy, and a streamlined and more efficient administration produced unwanted royal decrees regulating political and economic life.[5] The solidification of frontier-minded individuals in the north plus the rise of a prominent circle of Bexareños with their own ideas and interests, particularly in local matters, acted, by the early nineteenth century, to strain relations between the province and central government in Mexico City.

HIDALGO'S GRITO

In the last decades of the eighteenth century, New Spain began to seriously reassess its colonial standing. The Enlightenment and the American Revolution had stirred notions of freedom among many in New Spain, and, as mentioned, tighter controls over the colony's administration had bred discord among the upper classes. The masses, by this time, had come to associate the Spanish regency with callous misrule. When in 1810 a curate named Miguel Hidalgo y Costilla raised a cry for independence in Dolores, Guanajuato, on the *Diez y Seis de Septiembre* (September 16), folks from different classes rallied to his cause. But the war against bad government quickly assumed an ominous turn, becoming a social revolution of the lower classes against their Spanish oppressors, both native- and foreign-born.

Within weeks, therefore, of the *"Grito de Dolores"* ("Cry of Dolores"), Tejanos faced the dire choice of either joining or renouncing Hidalgo's movement. As in other corners of the Spanish empire, some considered insurrection an act of disloyalty, but others received it heartily. Hence, when a retired presidial officer named Juan Bautista de Las Casas headed a military uprising in Béxar to remove the few crown officials still there in January 1811, he attracted followers within the local presidio as well as among some of the less fortunate elements of the town's civilians, though some people of high station in the community also supported him firmly. The rebellion soon widened as patriots in other Texas settlements took up Hidalgo's struggle against royal authority.[6] However, Las Casas proceeded to confiscate property and cattle, jail people, and with sundry other acts estrange many important citizens, including many who had originally assisted him in his insurgency. Soon he faced a challenge from important rancheros troubled by his rash behavior.[7]

Therefore, on March 1, alarmists from the church, the military, and some of the influential ranching families of San Antonio succeeded in forming a counter rebellion and ousting Las Casas and recapturing control over the town. For his impudence, crown officials in Coahuila shot Las Casas in the back for treason, decapitated him, and forwarded his head to Béxar so that citizens could witness first-hand the punishment for taking up arms against royal power. Father Hidalgo, the major leader of the insurrectionary forces against the crown, met defeat on the battlefield near the city of Guadalajara the same month and suffered the same fate.[8]

Not all the distinguished families in San Antonio had supported the restoration of royalist influence in reaction to Las Casas. In August 1812, as a matter of fact, another group of Béxar leaders and ranchers welcomed one Bernardo Gutiérrez de Lara, who, claiming to be carrying on Hidalgo's dream of an independent Mexico (as New Spain was now called), entered Texas from Louisiana and seized Nacogdoches. From there, Gutiérrez de Lara and his Republican Army of the North (whose ranks included filibusters who were both Mexican and Anglo), marched toward Béxar and La Bahía, subduing both communities and raising their independence flag over the province in the spring of 1813.

Select families in Béxar endorsed Gutiérrez when he appointed a junta.[9] Ill advised deeds, however, swiftly put off many in the town as Gutiérrez committed atrocities in the region, including the execution of the royalist governor. To regain command of the province, crown representatives in the interior of Mexico directed Commandant General José Joaquín Arredondo to march into Texas and break the republican movement. In August 1813, Arredondo accomplished his mission and expelled the rebels. Through incarceration, the sequestering of private properties, and the arbitrary execution of suspected conspirators, the Spaniards had reasserted crown governance but further aggrieved the province's citizens.[10]

Several of the oldest rancho families of the province made their way to Louisiana to escape Arredondo's wrath. There, José Antonio Navarro, one of the Tejano ranchers turned refugee, and some of his peers survived as common workers near Opelousas, Attakapas, and Bayou Pierre. The wealthy ranchero Erasmo Seguín, who was accused of treason and had his property confiscated, suffered similarly in Louisiana. Others had taken to the wilderness. José Francisco Ruíz, for example, remained with Texas Indian tribes for several years. Many who did not succeed in reaching sanctuary met death at the hands of Arredondo's military men.[11]

Following Arredondo's purge, crown representatives lorded over Tejanos, eking out a survival from whatever abandoned fields and ranches could produce, by force of arms. Opportunistic individuals in the province made use of the chaos to confiscate property adjoining their own or to take a neighbor's belongings. Depredations by hostile Indians increased, adding to the turmoil and forcing landowners to practically abandon stock raising.[12] By 1821, when Mexico got its independence from Spain, the number of inhabitants in Texas had declined to about one-third of what it had been before Hidalgo's "Cry of Dolores." In East Texas, the nearly depopulated settlement of Nacogdoches struggled to remain in existence.[13]

La Independencia: Texas Under Mexico's Rule

On September 27, 1821, triumphant armies marched into Mexico City, marking the winning of Mexico's independence from Spain. For Tejanos, the change of sovereignties caused little disruption in accustomed behavior. The people of Texas passed into the new age with their identity intact and confident of their ability to affiliate themselves with the political and economic structure before them.

Among cultural accoutrements surviving into the 1820s without modification were many associated with rancho work. Riding gear that the Spaniards had borrowed from the Moors was still employed on Texas ranches, as were methods of handling stock, annual roundups that determined ownership of wild animals, the branding of cattle and horses, and, naturally, range vocabulary. The manner of working sheep similarly persisted, so that *pastores* (sheep herders) abided by customs and practices that had been in use since their forefathers arrived in Texas in the first expeditions of the 1710s.[14]

Aspects of the Iberian legal tradition also endured, such as those pertaining to women. In Mexican Texas (1821–1836), a woman retained the title to property she held at the time of matrimony; in the United States during the same era, the newlywed surrendered any such possession to her husband. Wives, furthermore, laid equal claim to assets earned while married; gains made during the marital state became the common property of the couple, and the husband could not dispose of that property without his spouse's consent. Society respected a woman's power to negotiate contracts and a widow's or unmarried daughter's right to handle her own estate.

Customs protecting debtors similarly persevered. The Spaniards had followed the tradition that held that working persons who were in debt could not, by demand of the creditor, be dispossessed of the means by which they earned their livelihood; thus work animals, as well as gear and other implements necessary to do one's job could not be confiscated except to indemnify the king or an overlord. Laws during the Mexican period in Texas acknowledged a common man's right to retain his tools, field animals, and even his land despite indebtedness.

The above cultural baggage passed not only from Spanish to Mexican rule, but to American domination of the province as Anglo Texans absorbed tenets of Spanish heritage after 1836. Texas ranch terminology even today preserves terms such as lariat (*la reata*), lasso (*lazo*), stampede (*estampida*), buckaroo (*vaquero*), cinch (*cincha*), and common loan words like mesquite, burro, and corral. The highly competitive American sport of rodeo traces its beginnings to the Iberian custom of performing an annual cattle roundup to clarify ownership. The Spanish legacy to post–1836 Texas is also apparent in the work methods and vocabulary of modern-day sheep and goat raisers.[15]

TOWN LIVING

During the years of Mexico's rule over Texas, Tejanos continued to live in the old localities of Central and southern Texas, surviving on their agrarian skills. But others preferred to reside in the three urban communities that had been established in the 1710s and 1720s: San Antonio, Goliad, and Nacogdoches. According to one census count, about 2,500 souls lived in the province in 1821.[16] But their numbers increased. Juan Almonte, who toured Texas in 1834 on a fact finding mission on behalf of the government in Mexico City, reckoned that San Antonio (and its rural environs) was home for about 2,400 Tejanos, Goliad 700, and Nacogdoches an additional 500. Victoria, a new settlement founded by Martin de León in 1824, had a population of 300 that year. To the south of these Central Texas towns lay the tenacious settlement of Laredo; approximately 2,000 people lived there in 1835.[17]

The towns were home to a coterie of skilled tradesmen and merchants, though by no means were these avenues to a life of ease. The former still found it difficult to find stable employment in a predominantly pastoral economy, while the latter, primarily in San Antonio, engaged chiefly in buying merchandise in Mexico—bedding, footwear, and dry goods—and selling it locally. Merchants generally descended from those having land, livestock, political power, and social prestige.[18]

Townfolk generally assumed efforts (through donations, for example), to provide schooling for their children when neither the government nor the church (which under both Spain and Mexico had a prerogative over such matters) could not fulfill their commitment to education. When and where they existed, schools relied on the Lancastrian system of education, a method which utilized advanced students to teach those in lower grades. Young charges learned the fundamentals of arithmetic, reading and writing, Catholic doctrine, and civics. But in a frontier society such as Texas's, the provision and maintenance of a sound educational system did not hold priority over matters of survival. Therefore children ordinarily went unschooled.[19]

Throughout the 1820s and 1830s, the church ministered to the souls living in Texas but, confronted with political and other assorted problems in the interior, never fully devoted proper attention to the province. It consistently failed to allocate sufficient funds for its Texas work; a result was a clergy that entered other avocations (ranching, teaching, and the like) to supplement earnings and meet the wants and needs of their parishes. Poorly tended to by the Catholic Church, Tejanos persisted in practicing a popular religiosity fashioned by their forefathers in New Spain, one which blended tenets of Catholicism with Mexican and Indian rites.[20]

RANCHING AND FARMING

Wild horses and cattle wandered freely throughout Central and southern Texas at this time. Neglect, violent storms, and Indian raids had dispersed many herds. As had their ancestors during the colonial period, rancheros around San Antonio tracked down mesteños as a source of livelihood, but the government intervened by enacting decrees that regulated the capturing, branding, marketing, and butchering of the wild herds.[21] To an extent, government regulation got in the way of the ranching industry's expansion, but Bexareños devised ways to make unreported beef sales to the local soldiers and families and even to covertly export herds to Louisiana and to places in Mexico south to the Rio Grande.[22]

In the trans-Nueces region there roamed additional cattle and horse stock, some of it tamed, much of it wild, but almost wholly available to men of enterprise. Since the late eighteenth century, grantees had struggled to found the ranching industry there: frequently by entrusting local cowhands to manage their affairs as they retreated to the safety of the river communities, sojourning back to inspect their ranching concerns as the occasions arose. Constant Indian attacks forced the area's pioneers to abandon their homes periodically, but their invariable return bore an increasingly successful claim to the region by the late 1820s. Town dwellers in Laredo during the same period similarly ventured into neighboring rural properties to establish ranches; these undertakings created new occupations for commoners and increased the landowners' benefits.[23]

Farming in Mexican Texas still remained as unappealing to Tejanos (for reasons previously given) as it had during the colonial years. What little of it existed amounted to subsistence horticulture. In San Antonio, Bexareños worked family-owned tracts, while more fortunate property owners cultivated vegetables, grains, fruits, and even cotton in irrigated fields. Any surplus agricultural products went to local markets. Rarely did the farms in Texas yield enough for exchange outside the province.[24]

SOCIETY

Socioeconomic condition and not race distinguished classes in Mexican Texas as it had before 1821. Government position, membership in a prominent family, business achievement, and land ownership might make one eligible for elite status. On the other hand, *peones* (commoners) who performed common labor and were of a mixed-blood or Indian stock constituted the lower stratum, though being a peon did not preclude one's rising in class since wealth, if acquired, could elevate the peasants to a higher social category.[25]

The elite, whose wealth by outside standards was not immense, tended to be literate, and they tried to provide for their children's education, sometimes sending them to Coahuila or hiring tutors. They held their own dances to which attendance by the poor was discouraged. During special occasions, the more privileged led ceremonial processions down the main streets or gave speeches at important events; such roles magnified their status as members of the upper class. Politically, it was the better established that expressed opinions; plain folks either voiced sentiments resembling those of their providers or remained detached from the realm of politics.[26]

WOMEN

Statutes specifying female political roles, men's attitudes toward women, and social norms governing female behavior passed sovereignties without modification. On the one hand, Tejanas retained those rights and privileges they had held during the colonial era, including the freedom to engage in their own ranching and other commercial activities. But they also continued to suffer from old disabilities. The male-oriented culture of the Tejanos discouraged political activism among women by barring them from holding office or using the franchise. Cultural dictates still subordinated women to men and attempted to confine them to the home. Societal norms also imposed a double standard of moral behavior: husbands could be unfaithful and escape censure, but an unfaithful woman incurred ostracism from frontier society and even the wrath of the law, which permitted confiscation of an adulteress's property. Marriages were not easily dissolved; indeed, the law could compel wives to stay in an unhappy union. Similar to other Western cultures of the era, women attended first to their husbands at meal time, then withdrew to eat apart.[27]

In this frontier atmosphere, women rendered a valuable service to society as wives and mothers who contributed to family stability. Most Tejanas lived out their lives on ranches and in the towns, trying their best to overcome adversity, family problems, isolation, and other forms of misery that plague humankind. They withstood travail with the support of neighbors and loved ones and contributed to society through altruistic activities, assisting men in business endeavors, and giving to the church in the form of voluntary services or donations.[28]

ANGLO AMERICANS ARRIVE IN TEXAS

Mexico not only inherited Spain's heritage but the old country's problems in the Far North. Texas, particularly, faced menacing Anglo Americans from the east who seemingly every year edged closer to the Sabine River. The nation was quite concerned about the Anglos' westward tide, but as of 1821, demographic forces in the Mexican interior still were not pressuring citizens to migrate north. After weighing different plans to augment the Tejano population, the new government in Mexico City finally opted to encourage European and United States immigrants to settle in the province in order to counteract threats posed by other national powers and Indians.

In so doing, Mexican leaders had continued an immigration policy begun in early 1821 when the Spanish crown granted to Moses Austin, a Missouri entrepreneur, a contract to settle three hundred Catholic families in the province. When Austin died that summer, his son Stephen accepted the agreement and founded a settlement on the Brazos River.[29]

SETTLEMENT AND REACTION

Tejano property holders had long dreamed of seeing their part of the Far North prosper. They saw excellent promise in the immigration program adopted by the state of Coahuila and Texas (when Mexico established a new government after achieving independence from Spain, Texas became a section of the state of Coahuila) in 1824, which invited settlers from the United States. Tejano leaders greeted Anglo arrivals warmly, for they hoped that large numbers of immigrants would offer protection from the region's roving Indian tribes and recovery from the general devastation created by the turmoil of the 1810s: the rancho economy would be resurrected, new lands turned into productive cotton fields, and commercial activity would be stimulated. For industrious Texas Mexicans, the new order would mean unbounded trade spreading to regions beyond the Rio Grande, to Coahuila, and even to Nuevo Mexico and the westernmost parts of the United States. Understandably, therefore, Bexareño entrepreneurs backed efforts to persuade the Mexican government to exempt the new arrivals from payment of such taxes as custom duties and tariffs. They also helped the new Anglo settlers to stave off abolitionist efforts.[30]

By the late 1820s, the Mexican immigration policies had, in the view of the national government, worked much too well, for the Anglo settlers had designs other than discharging their responsibility to protect the province from interlopers. In the eastern section of the province they had implanted their own way of life, broken agreements such as their promise to practice Catholicism (a condition upon which they had become Mexican citizens), and engaged in private land speculation and smuggling.[31]

In what may have been Mexico's first gesture to reverse a policy gone awry, President Vicente Guerrero in 1829 issued directives freeing all slaves throughout the country. But influential Tejanos teamed up with leading Anglo spokesmen such as Stephen F. Austin to win a temporary respite; after hearing the case for needed labor, the government opted not to apply the manumission decree to the province. The next year, however, Mexico turned to a more decisive course, passing the Law of April 6, 1830, to arrest immigration from the United States and curb the importation of African Americans under indenture contracts.[32]

Though a government receptive to Tejano and Anglo needs came to office in Mexico City in 1833, it lasted only until 1835 when Antonio López de Santa Anna assumed power in the capital. By then, some 35,000 Anglo Americans had streamed into the eastern areas of Texas, creating increased concerns in Mexico over the possibility of a separatist revolt in that area.[33]

THE ANGLO-TEXAN REBELLION, 1835–1836

Anglos, however, had always objected to stricter regulations regarding commerce in the gulf ports, collection of tariffs, abolitionist talk, and efforts to strengthen military forces in the province. In 1835, therefore, they joined the resistance erupting throughout Mexico against Santa Anna's regime. Texan troops clashed with Mexico's forces at San Antonio de Béxar from November through December. Tejanos assisted the Anglo Texans in this early effort, both as militiamen and civilians; among those Tejanos leading companies then were Captain Juan N. Seguín. Many of the families who had participated in the Mexican independence movement of the 1810s again aligned themselves with the concerns of the Texas region. On the other hand, numerous Tejanos, even among the social elite, sided with Mexico against the Anglo Texans. The majority of Tejanos, however, took a neutral stand on the hostilities.[34]

Determined to smother the Texas rebellion in the same manner as he had one in Zacatecas, Santa Anna (duly authorized by the Mexican congress) headed for Texas with a force of six thousand soldiers. Not all of Santa Anna's soldiers qualified as professionals, however: many were untrained conscripts, others political prisoners, and still others Mayan Indians who had been impressed into the military even though they lacked a command of the Spanish language.[35] The firearms with which Texas would be conquered, moreover, hardly ranked with the latest in weaponry. Cavalry units carried smoothbore muskets that had been acquired from the British after the English army had condemned them as obsolete; they had a range of some seventy-five yards. The operation was devoid of medical conveniences; the army included no trained physicians and only a minimum of essential medical paraphernalia.[36]

On February 23, 1836, the Mexican army arrived in Béxar. Santa Anna then laid siege to the Alamo, one of Béxar's old missions, in which Texan and Tejano volunteers led by William Barrett Travis had taken refuge. For several days Santa Anna prepared for the assault; meanwhile the volunteers inside the Alamo planned their defense. Finally, on March 6, at 5:30 A.M., Santa Anna ordered 2,400 of his men to attack and to give no quarter. But they found the Alamo a difficult fortification to crush: like other strongholds that the Spaniards had constructed, the mission's purpose was defense—indeed, its designers had positioned it on elevated ground so as to permit defenders a good view of would-be attackers rushing toward its eight- to nine-foot walls. Moreover, the Anglos inside the Alamo had already fortified it with twenty-one artillery pieces, making it the best equipped military installation between New Orleans and Monterrey, Mexico. Further, the Anglo defenders enjoyed an advantage in small weapons, possessing knives, handguns, and, most significantly, Kentucky long rifles which many used expertly.

As the Mexicans charged, the Alamo defenders greeted them with deadly fire. Downed immediately were those carrying ladders; consequently, the officers and the experienced soldiers behind them found it impossible to scale the high stone walls of the fortress. Meantime, the defenders used their guns and cannons with frightening accuracy. For the moment, the attack appeared to be on the verge of falling apart, but refusing to lose territory to the foreigners, Santa Anna called upon his reserve units to uphold the nation's integrity. As this wave attacked, however, it accidentally shot those amassed at the base of the walls. But eventually the remaining attack force scrambled up the ladders and into the Alamo. After more than an hour of combat the bloodshed had ended: all of the Alamo's defenders were dead and Santa Anna had lost some 500 to 600 men.[37] Only a few people inside the Alamo were spared from death. These included several family members of the six or so Tejanos who had elected to side with the Anglos, two Anglo Americans, Susannah Dickinson and her small child, and one African American, a slave owned by the slain William Barrett Travis.[38]

Four days prior to the fall of the Alamo, Anglo colonists had already decided upon a complete break with Mexico. At Washington-on-the-Brazos on March 2, 1836, three Mexican-descent persons were among the signers of the Declaration of Independence. One of the Texas signatories was Lorenzo de Zavala, a prominent liberal from Yucatán who had arrived in Texas to manage his real-estate holdings and escape Santa Anna's wrath. José Antonio Navarro and José Francisco Ruíz of Texas also signed the declaration; these two men had been among the Mexican oligarchs committed to fulfilling regional objectives through Anglo immigration. Swollen streams deterred another Tejano representative, Juan Antonio Padilla, from participating in the momentous gathering.[39]

Following his costly victory at Béxar, Santa Anna headed for East Texas to battle Sam Houston, who led the main Texan army. At San Jacinto, Santa Anna's army, which now numbered 1,500, engaged

Houston's force of 900, though from a position that ceded the foreigners an advantage: Santa Anna was enclosed on all sides, having Houston at his front, swamp terrain behind him, and part of the San Jacinto River to his right. At 4:30 P.M., Houston's units (which included a small company of Texas Mexicans led by Juan N. Seguín) launched a surprise maneuver that the Mexicans could not repulse. Instead, many of Santa Anna's men retreated in confusion, unable to regroup since so many of the veterans who might have been able to rally their subordinates because of their rank and battlefield experience had died at the Alamo. After eighteen minutes, therefore, Houston's army secured command of the Mexican camp. But the Anglos continued the onslaught into nightfall, slaying Mexicans who were fleeing into the prairie, the swamp, and the San Jacinto River. Santa Anna's army suffered some 600 deaths and 200 injuries; only eight Texans died, and twenty-five were wounded.[40]

Three weeks following the Battle of San Jacinto the Anglo Texans negotiated the Treaty of Velasco with Santa Anna wherein the defeated general conceded Texas independence and agreed to remove his army to Mexico beyond the Rio Grande. The congress in Mexico City disavowed the agreement, but Texas independence proved to be a fait accompli, since Mexico's army subsequently proved unable to retake the lost province.[41]

Viva México, Viva Texas

The war for Texas independence placed Texas Mexicans in a quandary. Initially, some Tejanos had contributed to the siege of Béxar in November and December of 1835, but that had been in consequence of cruel treatment before the hands of the local commander of Mexico's forces, Martín Perfecto de Cos, who compelled many men to perform menial tasks such as sweeping the streets and made the women bake tortillas for his troops. Additionally, he had impressed draft animals, wagons, and drivers and had destroyed people's homes on Béxar's outskirts to get a clearer view of any attacking Texan forces.

But the withdrawal of the Mexican troops from San Antonio hardly improved the Tejano lot, as the triumphant Anglos now occupying the town insisted that the local populace share their livestock, corn, beans, and other provisions. When Bexareños resisted, the Texans forced them to cooperate with the occupiers. Further, the Anglo soldiers eyed the Tejano citizens with suspicion, considering them potential spies, as the town residents had not been unanimous in backing the Texan army during the siege.

In Goliad, where an Anglo-Texan army had taken over the presidio in October 1835, Mexicans faced a similar predicament. The servicemen forced Texas Mexicans to barricade the plaza in Goliad and help them with sundry manual tasks. Lacking critical supplies, they commandeered Tejanos' property, including livestock, food, weapons, and tools. Many Texas-Mexican rancheros were stripped of their possessions in this way.

Also posing a dilemma to Tejanos, and explaining their vacillation towards the war for Texas independence, was the changing stand taken by the Anglo Texans; initially the Anglos had talked of maintaining certain rights and liberty but then declared for complete independence. While Tejanos supported the struggle for a democratic Mexico (as citizens had in other Mexican states such as Zacatecas and Coahuila), a complete break with the mother country was another matter. Additionally, Tejanos had misgivings about their status in the new republic, for they would certainly be transformed into a minority population.

The majority of Tejanos, however, had decided not to side with either belligerent. Though some may have sympathized with the Anglo cause and others might have preferred to defend the motherland from the threat of Anglo-American domination, they took to the countryside, opting to insure the safety of their loved ones instead. They assumed a tenuous neutrality throughout the crisis.[42]

MEXICAN AMERICANS

The Texas Constitution of 1836 proclaimed that all people living in Texas had automatically become citizens of the new republic at the moment the delegates at Washington-on-the-Brazos had declared independence. Thus did the subjects of Mexico become citizens of the new republic by the stroke of a pen. (Those absent at the time the document was signed but who later returned and desired citizenship could apply through normal procedures for naturalization.) Then, in 1845, residents of the Lone Star Republic received another new citizenship when the United States annexed Texas into the Union. The recognition of

U.S. citizenship applied to Texas Mexicans as well,[43] but by then Tejanos had already realized that the rights and privileges that accompanied citizenship in an Anglo-dominated society did not necessarily extend to them.

CHAPTER THREE

A New Citizenship:
Life in Anglo Texas
1836–1880

TEXAS MEXICANS in Central Texas faced cataclysmic changes following the Battle of San Jacinto. They now confronted the unfamiliar politics of the Republic of Texas, its laws, its social codes, its police authority, and the English language. Necessary for them was assuming a new citizenship while continuing their allegiance to the in-group culture that had taken shape over the centuries in New Spain.

In 1845, the Republic of Texas ceased, as sentiments for joining the United States led to annexation. Promptly, Mexico protested the loss of its wayward province. Efforts to negotiate a settlement proved fruitless, and an increasing American impulse for the acquisition of territories to the Pacific Ocean, a display of bravado on the part of Mexico, plus a multitude of other causes produced international hostilities in 1846 that lasted until 1848. Fought mainly in Mexico, but also along Mexico's far northern frontier, the War with Mexico ended with an American victory. In the Treaty of Guadalupe Hidalgo of February 2, 1848, the United States forced Mexico to recognize the Rio Grande as the southern boundary of Texas and to surrender the territories that make up the modern-day states of New Mexico, Arizona, California, and parts of Utah and Nevada. Mexico, in turn, got the United States to grant all of the rights of citizens to Mexican residents inhabiting the conquered lands.

For Texas Mexicans below the Nueces and westward beyond San Antonio, the war's end effected a repetition of earlier events in Central Texas. Mexicans in the newer frontiers experienced a cycle of land displacement, dilution of political power, occupational degradation, and racial subordination. The test for Tejanos in the aftermath of white intrusion in 1836 and 1845 would be devising the appropriate response essential for community survival. Transborder migrants who crossed the Rio Grande in subsequent years to pursue a destiny eluding them in Mexico would have to cope with a similar effort at adjustment.

On Three Frontiers

Between 1836 and 1850, the year in which the United States government took the first federal census in Texas, the Tejano population rose to more than 14,000. During the next thirty years, the Tejano community swelled approximately fivefold; the historian Roberto M. Villarreal estimates the number at 71,000 for 1880. Immigration accounted for much of the increase; migrants from Mexico comprised some 40 percent of the population total in 1850, 64 percent in 1860, and 61 percent in both 1870 and 1880.[1]

During the period, Texas Mexicans were clustered in three discernible population nodes. Some Tejanos still lived in the old Central Texas settlements, despite the war for independence and its aftermath, as well as in the new towns and on ranches that had been founded by Anglo Americans and European immigrants pushing west. After the Civil War, Mexican immigrants and Tejano migrant workers from below the Nueces filled in for exslaves on farmlands adjoining San Antonio to the east, and by the 1870s, Tejanos had became daylaborers on farms around Travis County and the Brazos district. The massive movement of Texas-Mexican farm hands into Central Texas would not occur, however, until the 1890s. In that part of the state therefore, Texas Mexicans in the nineteenth century occupied a minority status in a predominantly Euro-American populace.[2]

The setting in South Texas differed markedly. Mexicans there comprised a substantial majority. Many had moved into new communities that had been founded by Anglo Americans—among them Brownsville, Rio Grande City, Roma, and Corpus Christi—and into other sites established after the Civil War. But Anglos in the trans-Nueces controlled the region's economic and political foundations. Tejanos living

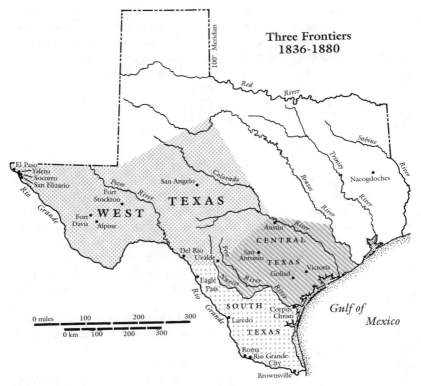

in South Texas, therefore, faced a quasi-colonial situation in which they were ruled by a small "foreign" element bent on directing the social life and development of the region.[3]

West Texas remained much of a hinterland as late as 1880, for American settlers did not start moving into the area west of the 100th meridian en masse until after the Civil War. During the 1870s, native-born Texas Mexicans and recent Mexican immigrants began entering newer communities such as Fort Davis, Fort Stockton, Alpine, and San Angelo, searching for work as shepherds, vaqueros, and farm hands. The El Paso Valley, however, had been home for Mexican-descent people since the 1830s when the Rio Grande shifted course and placed the Mexican villages of San Elizario, Ysleta, and Socorro on what became American territory following the signing of the Treaty of Guadalupe Hidalgo. Also, the beginnings of modern-day El Paso had been established in the 1850s when Anglo farmers and merchants appeared as part of the U.S. expansion westward to California (though the population of El Paso as of 1880 stood at about 700). Within the fifteen-year period between 1865 and 1880, however, enough Anglos had pushed into West Texas to make it a section in which each group comprised almost half the population.[4]

An Unneighborly Country

In these three regions, Central, South, and West Texas, Tejanos coexisted with unneighborly Anglo Texans who judged them to be a people of a lower caste. White society contemptuously thought Mexicans to be undeserving of equality with the white race, and mechanisms to insure Anglo supremacy abounded; they included political bossism, co-optation of the elites, a new and often racist police force, and the use of physical violence.

VIOLENCE

Violence directed against Mexicans in Texas had boiled over during the struggle for Texas independence and continued after the war. Suspected by Anglos of disloyalty and complicity in Santa Anna's atrocities, many Mexicans after the Battle of San Jacinto faced the choice of finding haven in Mexico, parts of the republic other than Central Texas (which in the summer of 1836 was still considered a war zone), or Louisiana. When the Tejano exiles returned in the late 1830s, most found their land confiscated or their cattle lost to Anglo claimants.[5] The residents of Béxar after about 1838, meantime, faced new perils, as whites arrived in the old community, turning San Antonio into "an open field for their criminal designs," as Juan N. Seguín, the city's mayor (1841–1842) put it.[6]

In the 1850s, flagrant attacks upon Tejanos persisted as xenophobia, politics, and economic rivalries mixed and incited racial antipathy. Communities in Central Texas, where slavery had existed since before the war for independence, expelled Texas Mexicans whom they suspected of aiding local slaves escape to Mexico and into freedom. In the 1850s, racial animosity also emerged out of competition between Tejano cartmen and Anglo freighters who competed to transport goods between settlements in the interior of the state and the gulf ports. In 1857, some of the Anglo freighters launched an all-out attack on the *arrieros*, waylaying the cartmen, destroying their cargoes, causing thousands of dollars in damages, and even killing some of the drivers. The so-called Cart War finally ended following the intervention of the Mexican minister in Washington, the American secretary of state, and some Texans who objected to the standstill in commerce and the blatant racist attacks on the Mexicans. Arrieros continued carrying goods to the coast after this, though the Civil War and subsequent economic changes after 1865 undermined their earlier monopoly.[7]

Similar clashes between the races spread to the territory below the Nueces River as Anglos penetrated the South Texas frontier for the first time. Anglo arrogance and Texas-Mexican rights became causes for contention. A by-product was the so-called "Cortina War," led by Juan N. Cortina, a scion of the old Tejano land grantees and a well-known leader in Brownsville. Cortina resented the ways in which the newly arrived Anglos in the lower border misused the judicial structure to divest Texas Mexicans of their property, challenge the old leaders for political supremacy, and compel people in the region to submit to new labor authority on their recently acquired range lands, all the while displaying a racist contempt for the Tejano masses. His embitterment reached a climax on July 13, 1859, at a Brownsville cafe. There, he witnessed the city marshal brutalizing a Mexican ranch hand; Cortina intervened on behalf of the Tejano, only to be insulted by the peace officer with an ethnic epithet. Cortina responded by firing on the lawman and injuring him.

Leaving an enraged Anglo population in the town, Cortina retreated to Mexico. In September 1859, he laid siege to Brownsville with a band of followers, threatened "death to the *gringos*," and in fact killed three of them, but was persuaded by Mexican authorities from Matamoros to relinquish his hold on the town. Regrouping at *Rancho El Carmen*, his mother's ranch situated west of Brownsville, he issued proclamations denouncing the Anglo presence in South Texas and vowing to seek redress for inflicted wrongs. Several efforts to dislodge him from his stronghold failed, and with every Cortina victory talk increased about expelling Anglos completely from the border. Texas Rangers and federal troops quelled the insurrection in early 1860, however, and chased Cortina into Mexico. Anglo Texans along the border then sought vengeance for Cortina's actions and waged a campaign of violence against suspected sympathizers. Retaliation involved the burning and looting of property as well as the killing of several Texas Mexicans.[8]

Following the Civil War, lynchings and other barbarities perpetrated against Tejanos found renewed expression. South Texas during the late 1860s and into the 1870s became a powderkeg of violence in the competition between profiteers from both sides of the border who sought to rustle cattle and mavericks from local ranches and the open South Texas range. Many suffered in the region, and much violence was inflicted on the innocent Tejano residents of the area who were implicated in the cattle raiding from Mexico. Atrocities reached such an ebb that the Texas Adjutant General supposed that few considered it a criminal act to kill Mexicans in that part of the state.[9]

Similar hate-motivated outbursts broke out in West Texas in the postbellum era as Anglo Americans migrated into that part of the state intent upon redeeming it for "civilization." A notorious clash occurred in the El Paso Valley over local salt lakes. For generations, the people of the area had mined the salt lodes located in the Guadalupe Peak, about one hundred miles east of El Paso. In the 1860s, a local ring of Anglo entrepreneurs begin conspiring to gain private title to the deposits. In the fall of 1877, anger over claims to the lakes erupted in a violent confrontation near San Elizario between the Mexican residents and members of the Salt Ring, bringing death and injury to both ranks. Renewed fighting broke out in December, but troops, Texas Rangers, and volunteer posses from New Mexico now arrived to pacify the region. The outsiders suppressed the popular local uprising, which came to be known as the "Salt War" by committing indiscriminate killings and other heinous acts. The people of the valley, therefore, lost their access to the salt beds.[10]

INTERETHNIC ACCOMMODATION

Whites also maintained authority over the mass of Texas Mexicans by securing alliances with prominent members of Tejano society (to what extent this faction avoided the aforementioned violence is difficult to measure). As noted in the previous chapter, social gradation characterized the Tejano community in the pre-Anglo period and this delineation withstood changes in nationhood. The fact is that throughout the nineteenth century, a segment of the Texas-Mexican population either retained parts of their old lands or acquired small parcels of real estate. In

the towns, furthermore, men and women with a business acumen profited by operating successful business concerns.[11]

Attracted by such material assets, Anglo men formed connections
with these Texas-Mexican elites, at least until about the 1870s, by
wooing available young women from prominent families. In San Antonio many succeeded to the extent that between 1837 and 1860, a minimum of one daughter from almost every well-to-do family in the city
had become the wife of an Anglo suitor. In South Texas, the newcomers
not only acquired valuable ranch property by marrying women from
landed families but incidentally acquired esteem and economic and political authority. With time, Anglos could capitalize on Tejano cultural
traditions to further their place in the upper stratum. Being a godparent
at an infant's baptism, sponsoring a youth at confirmation, or simply
being best man in a marriage made one a *compadre* to a family. Through
these ritual practices, the godperson's political clout among the Texas
Mexicans broadened.[12]

MANAGING THE MEXICAN VOTE

Anglos employed clever political mechanisms to control Tejano behavior at the polling booth. No law passed in the nineteenth century disfranchised the Tejano population, but whites took steps to deflect
potential threats to their political power base. Intimidation helped to
keep Tejanos in check, but beginning as early as the 1850s, political
bosses scornful of political procedure increasingly used what is termed
the controlled franchise. Under the stratagem used in South Texas, a
local *patrón*, or boss, dictated his resolve to Mexican "cross-mark patriots" or to noncitizens, influencing both with free food and alcohol on
the day of the vote, then directing them to cast their ballot for a specific
issue or individual.[13] Not infrequently, Anglo politicians solicited the
assistance of certain Texas Mexicans in their intrigues. Although these
lesser bosses were from the Tejano community, they ordinarily belonged
to well-off Texas-Mexican families motivated by the need to protect
their status and belongings through political collusion.[14]

THE LAW

Also effective in assuring Anglo sovereignty over Tejanos were certain
law-enforcement agencies. In the years following the Battle of San Ja-

cinto, the republic's soldiers had administered control, but Anglo law-men replaced army authority as time passed (some Mexican Americans did serve as members of the constabulary, though most of these men were related to one of the landed families). Peace officers symbolized white authority and often acted as the interpreters of the law. Linkages to other men of power, either locally or at the state house gave them commission to jail Mexicans if they thought it proper, organize posses to hunt down lawbreaking Mexicans, and even the right to execute insolent Tejanos (on the pretext of self-defense).[15] Then, *rinches* (the Texas Rangers) in the post–Civil War period came to bolster frontier law and often took enforcement into their own hands, applying the *ley de fuga* (law of flight) in their encounters with Texas Mexicans.[16]

WORKING THE OLD LANDS

After the war for Texas independence and the Mexican War, land grantees experienced formidable problems in retaining claims to their holdings. Rapacious Americans pressured Tejanos to sell their property. When the Tejano landowners refused to sell, they were often forcibly evicted. In Central Texas, Navarro and some of the relatives of Seguín had sold out by midcentury, and Seguín himself signed away what remained of his family's real estate in Wilson County in the 1870s, then moved to Mexico to join family members.[17] Also, Tejano landowners wrestled with the vagaries of the new American economy. Part of their dilemma, observes Professor David Montejano, stemmed from their outlook on the rancho. To Mexicans of South Texas, land sustained one's familial well-being and bestowed respect and status upon its owners. Comparatively, Anglo ranchers regarded land purchase as an investment, or as means to turn profits quickly. When a great demand for longhorns outside Texas boomed following the Civil War, the Mexican elite was illprepared to compete with the Anglo ranchers. Having neglected to invest in their estates, the rancheros were hard pressed to organize and finance their own cattle drives north. In desperation to supply the buying market, rancheros contracted with Anglo agents who bought their stock from them cheaply and then drove the herds to Kansas or Missouri where they sold it expensively.

Other forces contributed to the Tejano stockmen's losses. Barbed wire fenced off all the range land in South and Southwest Texas during the 1870s, yet few Tejano ranchers could muster the capital to buy their own supply. Nor did they have the cash (or access to loans) to pay taxes, improve their cattle breeds, survive droughts, or expand their grazing lands. Therefore, the financially overextended Tejano rancheros became severely vulnerable to downward spirals in demand for beef, or, for that matter, even erratic weather conditions. Montejano's research shows that Mexican land sales to Anglos with available credit rose during economic slumps.[18]

Life for laborers on the ranches of South Texas generally reflected a well-defined agrarian order. Despite the Mexicans' acknowledged ranching skills, Anglos considered them a lazy people, imputing to them a weakness for indolence and revelry, perhaps as a means of justifying Tejano exploitation.[19]

But forced subservience did not stifle the Tejano will to work the range the Mexican way. "When Mexicans could no longer ride for themselves," notes the historian Jack Jackson, "they rode for others, passing on their knowledge and customs to subsequent generations of 'buckaroos.'"[20] This range culture, of course, harked back to Spain, and Tejanos applied it to the Anglo border ranches which functioned so successfully under American rule. When sheep ranching grew in the Rio Grande Plain after the Civil War and then spread towards West Texas, Texas Mexicans applied their time-tested practices to that industry as well.[21]

Anglos also presumed themselves the Mexicans' social superiors, even as they accepted the pre–Mexican War paternalistic and patriarchal practice of maintaining the labor force through a mutual understanding in which workers exchanged their toil for certain amenities. Most men and women on the Texas ranches continued to look to a patrón for the necessities of life, among them a place to live and wages (either cash, or, as was more often the case with the vaqueros, clothing, ammunition, tobacco, and other provisions). Despite this paternalism, a clear understanding existed between the white rancher and the Mexican-American ranch hands: Mexicans were to be deferential, assent to their social inferiority, and the men were to avoid mixing with white women.[22]

THE BARRIOS

Like most Texans, Texas Mexicans were predominantly rural dwellers. As of 1850, only 16 percent of the total Tejano population resided in municipalities. At no time during the nineteenth century did the number of Texas-Mexican urban denizens exceed 25 percent.[23]

Several observations may be made regarding late-nineteenth-century urban life for Tejanos. First, most of them lived amidst poverty and urban blight. As Texas urbanized in the last half of the nineteenth century, jobs in trade, transportation, and manufacturing opened up, but Anglos were the primary beneficiaries. Left for Tejanos were jobs of an unspecialized nature which offered little chance for material advancement.[24] Also, most Mexicans resided in neighborhoods of their own founding, generally because towns after 1836 were Anglo developments, built close to some important ranch, a frontier fortification, or another commercial center.

In the *barrios* (Mexican neighborhoods), furthermore, the racial order of the countryside that associated Tejanos with backwardness and inferiority applied with only slight modification. In Texas cities, the result of the ethnically divided neighborhoods meant that the barrios as a district received a lack of attention from city officials, including the police, disregard from civic leaders, and disrespect by the common citizenry. But at the same time, the Mexican quarter acted as a focal point for Tejano life. In that setting, Tejanos preserved in-group culture, political ideologies of various persuasions took form, Catholic priests and Protestant clergymen ministered to the faithful, and merchants sold their stock and delivered services in ways familiar to their patrons.[25]

Community in American Texas

Like their counterparts in other regions of the United States, especially the northern cities where immigrant groups tended to settle, Tejanos in the ranching areas and the urban barrios retained components of Mexico's culture. After all, Mexico-born people constituted a majority of the overall Tejano population as late as 1880. Gradually, however, a fusion of Mexican and Anglo ways within Tejano culture occurred.

A SYNCRETIC CULTURE

Linkages to Mexico in Tejano culture are evident in language, a patriotic loyalty to the old country, an aesthetic appreciation for Mexico's heritage, housing types, foods, folklore, religious beliefs, and ways of entertainment. Thus, Tejanos built their homes in the form of jacales and adobe as they had on both the Mexican and Texan frontiers. They partook of *frijoles, tortillas, tamales, chiles, cabrito* (kid goat), and *nopalitos* (leaves of cactus) as they had for generations. Tejanos remained faithful to many Catholic beliefs and customs, though some accepted the proselytizing of Protestant missionaries. Ethnic festivals including commemorations of Mexican national holidays, such as the *Diez y Seis de Septiembre* and the *Cinco de Mayo* (May 5)—the date on which the forces of Mexico repelled a major French invasion in 1862—kept up patriotic Mexican sentiments. Spanish-language news publications informed readers of current events in Mexico, educated immigrants about American society, and incidentally preserved the native language. Newspapers first appeared in San Antonio in the 1850s (actually, a hiatus in publication had existed since the 1820s), then in select cities throughout the state after Reconstruction. Texas Mexicans also established, during the 1870s, benevolent associations that offered barrio members and their families assistance in times of unemployment, destitution, sickness, or death. These societies went by such names as *Club Recíproco* (Reciprocal Club) and *Sociedad Mutualista Benito Juárez* (Benito Juárez Mutualist Society).[26]

The building of the Tejano community in Texas also involved syncretization, however. In everyday affairs, Texas Mexicans had common interchange with their employers, merchants, policemen, and other agents of white America. They also interacted with Catholic and Protestant churches, public organizations, and schools. From necessity, some learned the English language, though not necessarily fluently. Those piqued by politics joined the debate over controversies of the state and nation. Common men and women incorporated Anglo-American motifs into popular folklore; *corridos* (folk ballads) made mention of American personalities such as Ulysses S. Grant, for example. Similarly, American national holidays, among them Washington's Birthday, Independence Day, and even the U.S. Centennial in 1876, came to be observed as part of a group consciousness.[27]

SOCIAL DIVERSITY

Just as the community was ethnically diversified, so it was economically and socially. Most Tejanos lived as members of the lower stratum, but a small part of the community fared better. Among them were landowners who traced their ancestry to the pre–1836 era and still retained portions of their property. A handful could be found in Central Texas after the Civil War, though the great majority of Tejano land grantees had by then lost their possessions to Anglos. Rancheros in South Texas, in comparison, survived with small parcels of land, though in that region also most of the valued estates had passed into Anglo hands by the means previously described. By being resilient, the remaining Tejano stockmen either beat the odds in times of depression by commercializing and acclimating themselves to the new market, or used racial intermarriage to buffer the impact of the Anglo presence on their economic standing.[28] Along the border region, therefore, stretched several Tejano-owned ranchos—examples include *Laguna Seca* of Don Macedonio Vela, *Randado* of Hipolito García, and *Los Ojuelos* of Dionisio Guerra—which made good in the cattle boom of the 1870s and even expanded after that era.[29] The success of these ranches set their owners apart from the bulk of South Texas Tejanos who were serving as ranch hands and daylaborers.

Also above the general caste of Tejano *obreros* (laborers) was a mercantile group that managed upstart business establishments. After the War with Mexico, members of the South Texas elite used already established economic networks in Texas and across the Rio Grande to their advantage. In the 1850s and after, they reaped profits from the trafficking of industrial goods going into Mexico from the United States and from agricultural products entering Texas from south of the border.[30] Meanwhile, some Mexican immigrants with fortitude devised means to start up modest business ventures and keep them afloat. Additionally, a corps of Tejano professionals, modest in size, evolved as settlements expanded in the post–Civil War years. Teachers, newspaper editors, physicians, druggists, and attorneys, as well as government officials serving as peace officers, sanitary inspectors, or custom collectors in the border areas augmented this middle class.[31]

As under Spain and Mexico, community members acknowledged social distinctions. Actually, the well-to-do preferred aloofness, and thus created their own circle of clubs and sponsored exclusive social affairs. Naturally, they lived commensurate with their status; they owned comfortable and well-kept homes and dressed more fashionably than most Tejanos.[32]

POLITICAL ISSUES AND TEJANOS

Ethnic variation and social differentiation in turn influenced the political posture that Tejano political activists took on matters of relevance to their lives and the people they represented. However, Anglos sought to limit Tejano suffrage, life in ranchos and barrios isolated Tejanos from politics, and as a group, moreover, Tejanos suffered from a bevy of political liabilities: a smaller proportion of Mexicans than Anglos qualified to vote because females in the Tejano population outnumbered males; the average age among Tejanos was lower than among whites; foreign-born status made many ineligible to practice the franchise; and high rates of illiteracy in English deterred many from the polls.[33]

Nonetheless, Tejanos evinced passion in deliberating the political and socioeconomic topics of the times: as expected, they espoused diverse, even conflicting positions. Tejanos joined the politics of the Republic of Texas as officeholders, though these were primarily the oligarchs from the Béxar region who had previously served in government under Mexico. Among them were José Antonio Navarro and Juan Seguín. The former went on to win local and state office several times, while the latter, a hero of the Battle of San Jacinto, found himself exiled from Texas in the 1840s for allegedly switching his allegiance to Mexico.[34]

The turmoil of the 1850s, the Civil War, and Reconstruction engrossed Tejanos in affairs of immediate pertinence to the community. In 1855–1856, Bexareños succeeded in helping defeat the Know-Nothing party which ran on an anti-immigration, antinaturalization, and anti-Catholic platform. Though the ideological postures assumed on political issues varied as much within the Tejano community as they did elsewhere in Texas, Tejanos were mostly sympathetic to Democratic party principles. When the party split into two competing factions in the late 1850s over the question of secession, there were Tejanos in both camps. When war erupted in 1861, oligarchs like Navarro and Santos Benavides of Laredo (who had managed to retain property and political influence) sided with the Confederacy while Cortina, who had taken refuge in Mexico following his defeat by Texan forces in 1860, allied himself with the Union cause. He waged guerrilla war on Confederate forces and used the chaos of war in an effort to forcibly subvert the presence of those Anglos wanting to encroach on the lands, the politics, and economy of South Texas.[35]

Like their elite counterparts, common folks took adversarial sides during the Civil War. Although the mass of Tejanos could not identify with the philosophical origins of the war, approximately 3,400 Tejanos participated in the conflict, according to the historian Jerry Don Thompson. Some 950 Tejanos joined the Union ranks, about 2,500 the Confederate forces. Aside from action in the trans-Nueces (where many preferred to serve in order to watch over the well being of their families), Tejanos fought in significant engagements in New Mexico, as well as in Tennessee, Virginia, and other states east of the Mississippi.[36] During the time of Reconstruction (1865–1876), political factions clashed on the question of rights for the freedmen, sometimes as heatedly as did their Anglo cohorts who split on the issue along Conservative and Radical lines.

Following the Civil War, Tejano incumbents (most of whom were associated with families having lucrative business and ranching interests) occupied numerous local offices, ranging from county commissioners to collectors, assessors, and treasurers. This was especially the norm along the border, as well as in the El Paso Valley. Tejanos even earned appointments or won elections to offices in counties being newly created in West Texas during the 1870s.[37] The commitment of such politicians to advancing the lot of the Mexican-American population varied from indifference to firm commitment.

José Antonio Navarro, perhaps the best known spokesman of the antebellum era, practiced politics driven by the ambition to see his region (Béxar) prosper economically (as he had during the Mexican era), by a nationalistic passion for the land of his birth (Texas), and by his awareness of white racial intolerance of Tejanos. Since the days of Stephen F. Austin, Navarro had developed linkages with powerful Anglo-American leaders, and between 1836 and 1871 when he died, he had signed the Texas Declaration of Independence, attended and participated in the constitutional conventions of 1836 and 1845, won election and served in the Congress of the Republic of Texas in 1838–1839 and again in 1846–1849, and supported the secessionist movement in Texas and later the South. Simultaneously, however, Navarro did not forsake the cares of Tejanos. The umbrage he took at the Constitutional Convention of 1845 at efforts to disfranchise Tejanos attests to his interest in protecting Mexican rights.[38]

Analogous is the career of Santos Benavides. A border-region politician who accommodated readily to American institutions following the Mexican War, Benavides occupied various political offices in Laredo and

Webb County in the 1850s, assisted Anglo military forces in suppressing the Juan Cortina disturbance in 1859, then fought on the side of the Confederacy. Serving in the state legislature between 1879 and 1885, Benavides sought to be nonpartisan in ethnic matters while he worked to modernize the border region. Reputedly, his political comportment earned him high marks among Anglo-Texan colleagues in the legislature.[39]

Bolder in affirming political convictions was Cortina who forcefully resisted the Anglo-American presence on the border. During the Cortina War, he professed to be championing Tejano rights and in his statements issued from *Rancho El Carmen*, inveighed against the Anglos' systematic expropriation of Tejano lands and the mistreatment of Texas Mexicans simply because of their nationality. He had threatened the extermination of the foreigners and had met them courageously on the battlefield. As a *caudillo* (regional strongman) in Tamaulipas during the 1860s and 1870s, Cortina warred against the border Anglos by coordinating cattle raids into South Texas. Force remained his political style, whether to defend fellow Tejanos, uphold his character and rights, or perhaps to advance his personal fortunes.[40]

A MARGINAL PEOPLE

Throughout much of the nineteenth century, the Mexican population in Texas struggled as a people in the margin of the dominant society. Government, schools, private institutions, and social agencies neglected them. The Catholic Church and Protestant denominations provided spiritual guidance but launched no efforts to achieve Tejano equality. Agrarian labor leaders dismissed Tejanos during the fledgling unionizing drives of the 1870s. Ranchers and farmers ignored notions about fair wages and treatment for their Mexican hands.

Treated as stepchildren, Tejanos sought to work out their own survival in poverty-stricken neighborhoods or on ranches. Actually, in some ways many Mexicans may have preferred their own separate sphere, for in segregated areas, familiar and comforting amenities could be practiced and enjoyed beyond the distrustful eye of outsiders. Indeed, Tejanos, like European immigrants of the same era, resisted Americanizing influences. But many Tejanos rejected their marginal status, also. They sought a life beyond the confines of the semiautonomous enclaves and displayed a resolve to join the mainstream. Barrio merchants and rancheros pushed to integrate their businesses into the larger economy. Parents enrolled their children in schools. Newspapers and benefit societies encouraged Tejano community members to stay abreast of local matters. Political leaders tried to find solutions to issues affecting the community. Anglos might have preferred a docile proletariat, but the Tejano will to improve the human condition produced an assertiveness that influenced the course of Texas history.

CHAPTER FOUR

Mexican Americans and Inmigrantes in a Modernizing Society 1880–1910

IN numerous ways, life in the last decades of the nineteenth century resembled that of the period before 1880 for Texas Mexicans. Racial attitudes persisted in virulent forms. Injury, death, or insult of a white by a Tejano, for example, invited certain wrath upon the entire Tejano community. When in June 1901 the farm renter Gregorio Cortéz shot a local sheriff near Kenedy in Karnes County, the Tejano fled towards Mexico knowing that he faced summary lynch law, even though he had killed the lawman in self-defense. Before being caught a few days later, he became the target of one of Texas's most massive manhunts, with those who had assisted Cortéz to escape suffering threats, imprisonment, and, in one notorious case involving an innocent thirteen-year-old boy, torture.

Into the early twentieth century, lynchings remained a method of racial control. In November 1910, Anglo vigilantes in Rocksprings went to the local jail, took Antonio Rodríguez (accused of killing a white woman on a ranch near the town), and burned him alive. In a similar case of impulsive action, a white mob in Thorndale beat fourteen-year-old Antonio Gómez to death in 1911 for killing a German Texan in a fight. They then dragged his corpse through the streets of town behind a buggy.

The tense nature of Anglo-Tejano relations even produced violent demonstrations. A handful of race riots erupted in the southern and western sections of the state in the 1880s and 1890s in which Tejanos reacted angrily to individual cases of harassment or to some act of injustice perpetrated upon the community. The most frightening riot occurred in Rio Grande City in 1888 when local Mexican residents sought to make amends for the Anglo shooting of the newspaper man Catarino Garza who had been editorializing against local Anglo law officers suspected of lynching Mexicans in the area. Hysteria gripped Anglo communities throughout the region as Tejanos seemed to be "loose" on the border, though they mainly sought the capture of Garza's assailant who had taken refuge in a local military post. Not much in the form of property destruction or loss of life actually occurred, and the "rioting" passed after a few days. Garza recovered to resume his career as an activist journalist in South Texas.[1]

Other aspects of Anglo-Tejano relations appeared out of place in a modernizing age. Political bosses still manipulated Mexican voters. Movements to disfranchise Tejanos culminated in a federal courtroom in 1896 in the case of *In re Ricardo Rodríguez* when two lawyers petitioned a San Antonio judge, although unsuccessfully, to deprive Mexicans of the vote on the reasoning that they descended from Indian blood.[2] On the landed estates of South Texas, ranch hands earned their keep under labor arrangements which were throwbacks to the Spanish-Mexican era.[3]

Texas Society in Transition

But there existed little doubt among all Texans that the period of the 1880s through the 1910s was one of transformation. For one thing, commercial farming replaced cattle ranching as the most common rural livelihood. Since the 1860s, Anglo Americans had been moving into new areas of the state—towards the Cross Timbers, West Texas, and the Panhandle—to establish new farms. There followed a general pattern of land transfer from ranches to farms across the state during the 1870s as the age of the cattle kingdom waned. A similar turn away from ranching occurred in South Texas, where the majority of Tejanos resided, as Anglo farmers from other parts of the United States began arriving in the region during the 1890s to supplant the old nineteenth-century ranch society. The farm revolution in the Lower Rio Grande Valley did not unfold until the first decade of the twentieth century, however.[4]

Also indicative of the new historical age was the diversification of the industrial sector of the economy. Railroads arrived in the state in the 1870s and took Texas in new directions. As it linked one town with another, the iron rail gave new life to cotton-growing gins and other agricultural pursuits and furthered newer industries such as lumber in the Piney Woods of East Texas. Manufacturing also came into its own during this time, and by 1900 the value of the state's manufactured products had reached unprecedented levels. But this still was not the end of the continued diversification, for wildcatters tapped the huge Spindletop pool (near Beaumont) in 1901. As other discoveries followed, they spurred new oil-related businesses.

Further separating the late nineteenth and early twentieth centuries from the older days were trends toward urbanization, although Texas remained basically agricultural. Houston evolved as a point of debarkation for cotton going to the northeastern United States and even Europe. San Antonio experienced immense population growth and economic prosperity with the arrival of the railroad—new buildings featuring modern architectural styles now spread outwardly from the city's downtown district.[5] El Paso grew into a major site for mining, livestock, tourism, and international trade.[6] In the early 1880s, train connections brought Laredo a new telephone system, paved thoroughfares, the English-language *Laredo Times*, as well as new government and mercantile buildings. Brownsville began modernizing when the St. Louis, Brownsville, and Mexico Railway reached the border city in 1904. In North Texas, the twin cities of Dallas and Fort Worth acted as a commercial center for regional goods heading to markets out of state.[7]

The new age was also different in its politics. The reform wing of the Democratic party, for one, took on new crusades, among them efforts to effect change in the corrupt world of big business, prison life, and the condition of the public schools. During the early part of the twentieth century, progressives took up further reforms, working to modernize eleemosynary institutions, cleanse society by prohibiting the sale and consumption of alcohol, grant women the right to vote, and eliminate abuses by politicians. By the early 1910s, good government leagues waged drives to alter the old ways of running city and county business in the lower border, where machine politics had reigned for decades.[8]

THE TEXAS-MEXICAN GENERATION

At least two major features distinguished the Texas-Mexican generation living in the period circa 1880–1910 from the preceding one: the size and origin of the population and a more participatory role for Tejanos. In the first case, the Mexican-American community increased perceptively. In 1880, according to Roberto M. Villarreal, the total Texas-Mexican population (including those of foreign birth) numbered 71,000. This increased to 105,821 in 1890, to 164,974 in 1900, and then to 279,317 in 1910. In 1880, the percentage of native-born Texas-Mexicans was 39 percent of the total population, but ten years later this standing had been elevated to 51 percent and the pattern continued thereafter. In 1900, 57 percent of the Texas-Mexican population claimed the United States as their country of birth, and in 1910, 55 percent did so.[9]

As had been the case before 1880, Tejanos predominantly peopled three regions: in 1900, about 46 percent of the Mexican-American population resided in South Texas below the Nueces River, 36 percent lived in Central Texas, and the remaining 18 percent were situated in a section of the state west of the Hill Country, including El Paso.[10] But by the last decades of the nineteenth century, Mexicans were advancing in increased numbers towards new terrains. They settled on Central Texas farms, renting alongside Anglo- and African-American tenant farmers. Migrant farm workers pushed towards Wharton (southwest of Houston in Wharton County) and as far east as the cotton lands adjacent to the Sabine River.[11] In the early years of the twentieth century, these migrant workers traveled in family groups by train and wagons to other parts of the state searching out the bountiful cotton fields in their struggle for survival.[12]

The second thing to be discerned during this time was an upturn in the Tejano community's involvement in regional, economic, and political activities. Several things may explain this. The rise of communities in South Texas and West Texas made positions available on town councils, police forces, and in public works. The fact that the majority of Texas Mexicans were of native birth meant that the community had an increased familiarity with American affairs; schools, churches, and other mainstream agencies helped Tejanos take advantage of new opportunities being opened up by a modernizing society. Lastly, Anglo Americans may have encouraged such a participation, ironically as part of the apparatus of control: Tejanos could minister to the growing population of Texas Mexicans in physically separated areas, so long as they did not disturb the Anglo society.

CONTINUED FRAGMENTATION

The transition occurring in late-nineteenth- and early twentieth-century Texas gave impetus to a fledgling middle class. This element within the Mexican-American community had remained more or less stagnant since midcentury; census figures for the period 1850 to 1900 show the group to have barely expanded. Indeed, during the last two decades of the nineteenth century, the percentage of Tejano farmers and stockraisers in the total Tejano population declined, from 12.1 percent and 4.2 percent to 8.6 percent and 0.7 percent, respectively. On the other hand, however, slight increases occurred in the number of Tejanos dealing in trade and transportation during the same period (7.0 percent to 7.6 percent) and in the number of Tejanos in the manufacturing and mechanical category (7.3 percent to 9.6 percent). Even as modernization dislodged many Tejanos from specific livelihoods, the process ushered in new possibilities. Census figures show that a relatively higher percentage of literate Tejanos found employment in trade, transportation, manufacturing, and mechanical occupations while illiterate workers predominated in the general labor sector.[13]

The late 1800s and early 1900s witnessed an increase in Tejano participation in the state's business fields. The urbanization of San Antonio, El Paso, Laredo, Corpus Christi, and other Texas cities naturally stimulated economic activity in Tejano sections, and natural reproduction in and recent immigration to the neighborhoods increased the number of customers demanding goods and services. Merchants, therefore, found themselves more involved with Anglo middlemen, negotiating with wholesalers for needed merchandise. As the mercantile establishments expanded, small shopkeepers such as watchmakers, jewelers, and grocers had to develop ties with the local power structure, arranging for things such as police and fire protection and necessary business licenses. More ambitious entrepreneurs formed links to state and national markets.[14]

Also involved in the economics of the age were landowners in South Texas, most of whom resided in ranch counties such as Zapata, Duval,

Starr, and Webb.[15] During this period several of them engaged in inter-state transactions of stock: some imported cattle and poultry from Kentucky, others sold beef to places as far away as Chicago, the Indian Territory, and Kansas City, Missouri. In West Texas, Tejanos also ran successful ranch operations, though not the equals of those in South Texas. Alongside the rancheros were Tejano farmers who experimented with new irrigation and cotton-growing techniques.[16]

The good fortunes of the entrepreneurial class, however, did not filter down to the whole of the community. The bulk of the Mexican-American population lived apart from mainstream institutions, with many families mired in poverty. This impoverished condition in part reflected the Tejanos' particular disadvantage, but it also mirrored the times. The great majority of Texans in this period—of every national origin—struggled with a hard life, working as small (often tenant) farmers and ranch hands, day workers, or as part of an urban (industrial) proletariat.

POLITICS OF DIVERSITY

Increased political animation also marked the years from the late nineteenth century to the early 1900s, most notably in, but not necessarily restricted to, South Texas. As new towns sprouted or old ones expanded, they required officials to oversee civic services, and Tejanos joined the competition for those positions. Racism, political powerlessness, and restricted opportunities for advancement became unifying and motivating forces that stirred Texas Mexicans into action. Urban problems emerged as points for debate, and reform-minded Texas Mexicans joined the discussion. The new era, therefore, found descendants of the old families and upstart newcomers from different social standings playing spirited roles in community affairs. Commonly, they were part of the machines of power brokers such as Jim Wells, a Cameron County political boss, but others belonged to independent groups grappling with the issues of the day.

Hot rhetoric on the stump (in Spanish, but sometimes in English) typified political campaigning in Cameron, Starr, Webb, and other counties of South Texas. In Laredo, and in Duval County, Mexican Americans joined the *guaraches* (sandals) and the *botas* (boots) in clashes of local importance. These were local factions whose names had little to do with representing constituents of different class standings as their labels (poor vs. rich) might suggest. In reality, the former represented the ranks of the old guard that had dominated politics since the 1850s, while the latter appealed to newer elements in the region wanting electoral reform.

In these counties Mexican Americans had consistent success in electing public officials from the 1880s through the early 1900s. Tejano campaigners were visible at almost all levels of local politics; their attendance at grass-roots conventions even impacted on processes outside South Texas by determining who would represent them at the congressional, senatorial, and state conventions.[17]

Intense political action was also evident in El Paso and its surrounding valley communities, such as San Elizario, Ysleta, and Socorro. In the late nineteenth and early twentieth centuries, Tejanos worked resolutely for a political voice in El Paso County and indeed won compromises from the Anglo Democratic ring. They retained posts, for example, in the county commissioners' court. Among the incumbents was Octaviano A. Larrazolo, a district attorney who moved to New Mexico later and served as that state's governor. Tejano politicians in far West Texas settlements kept informed by attending the county conventions of the two major parties.[18]

The fate of San Antonio Tejanos differed strikingly from those in South Texas and the El Paso region. As of the last decades of the nineteenth century, Bexareños filled a few city offices. Then occupancy withered amidst a rapidly increasing Anglo population (by 1900, San Antonio had grown into the largest city in the state) and their efforts to disfranchise Tejanos and to subdue their occupational ambitions.[19]

Tejano politicians also took stock of the possibilities available under political bossism. While on the one hand they used the arrangement for self-aggrandizement, to protect their vested interests, and to see to the preservation of business and regional needs, they also utilized boss rule to derive benefits for their communities. Through organized pressure, especially where they outnumbered Anglos, Tejanos effectively persuaded political rings to concede them patronage appointments. Additionally, Tejano politicians worked with bosses to assist community members when encountering legal problems, facing personal dilemmas such as those arising from the death of a loved one, or going through crises as a result of natural disasters.[20]

Among the most prominent Mexican-American politicians serving during this era was J. T. Canales. Between 1905 and 1910, Canales served as the representative for Cameron, Hidalgo, Starr, and Zapata counties in the Texas House of Representatives. In that capacity, he voted for numerous progressive measures, among them education, judicial, and tax reform, modernization of irrigation laws, and the creation of a State Department of Agriculture.[21] Another person who exerted wide influence in South Texas politics was Manuel Guerra. Fluent in English and astute in business techniques, he settled in Roma in the 1870s to care for a new business and to administer the Guerra properties in Starr County. During the mid–1880s, he created a political base in Roma, and until 1915, when he passed away, Guerra used his post on the Starr County Commissioners' Court to rule over county matters.[22]

WORKING-CLASS ACTIVITY

Severe working conditions, low pay, and limited opportunity for advancement prompted Tejano laborers to take action by launching organizing drives for self-improvement. Though Anglo labor leaders did not aggressively recruit among minorities, working-class Tejanos, individually and collectively, attached themselves to receptive labor unions in an effort to combat their impoverishment or enhance the general well-being of their communities.

Surprisingly, such alliances developed early outside South Texas. In 1886, Mexicans living in Galveston joined one of the first labor organizations in Texas, the Screwmen's Benevolent Association, and in Central Texas the Texas Knights of Labor courted San Antonio Tejanos for incorporation into industrial unions, although these overtures appear to have been brief.[23]

Strikes involving Tejanos similarly erupted in regions far beyond the trans-Nueces. The first significant strike that included Mexican-American participation occurred in the Texas Panhandle: this was the well-known cowboy walkout of 1883. A man named Juan A. Gómez ostensibly made up part of the leadership for he signed a document listing the cowhands' demands upon the ranch managers.[24] El Paso was also the scene of organized labor activism in the early years of the twentieth century. There, some two hundred construction workers at the El Paso Electric Street Car Company struck in 1901 for an increase in pay, as did smelter workers in the city in 1907, both unsuccessfully however.[25] In North Texas, Tejano miners from Thurber engaged in work protest during the 1890s, and railroad strikers of the Texas and Pacific Company in Thurber, with the support of the United Mine Workers, won a salary increase and shorter working hours in 1907.[26]

In Laredo, Tejano workers voted to affiliate themselves with the American Federation of Labor (AFL) when that national organization undertook a program to integrate Mexican Americans living in the Southwest into its ranks. In the city, Tejanos in the railway shops had organized Federal Labor Union (FLU) No. 11,953 in 1905. A year later, with an AFL charter on hand, the FLU launched a strike against the Mexican Railway Company (this connected Laredo with lines extending north to San Antonio and east to Corpus Christi) for better wages. But railroad management employed strikebreakers and court injunctions to weaken the walkout. While the workers won concessions early in 1907, the company relocated across the Rio Grande to Nuevo Laredo.[27]

Mexico in Texas

A majority of Texas Mexicans held the traditions and customs of Mexico dear, and they continued to draw upon their immigrant heritage (others clung to the past out of contempt for the behavior of Anglo Texas) in isolated ranch settlements and segregated enclaves. Furthermore, Mexican nationals continuously crossed into Texas pursuing seasonal work on farms and in developing cities, and by the late 1890s and early twentieth century, farmers actively recruited seasonal workers at several border stations.[28] As the immigrants shuttled between countries, they reinforced old cultural standards in communities where they settled.

HISTORICAL FORCES AND IMMIGRANTS

Since a significant portion of Tejanos were new arrivals from Mexico, they helped to maintain the whole group's cultural contact with the old country. Major influxes of people from below the Rio Grande started in the 1890s. In 1880 and 1890, 61 percent and 49 percent respectively of the Tejano community reported their status as being of foreign birth. In 1900, 43 percent of the total Texas-Mexican population of 164,974 reported to have been born in Mexico, but combined with first generation Tejanos, immigrants and their offspring constituted 86 percent of the

Mexican-American people in Texas. Of the total 279,317 Tejanos counted in the census of 1910, 45 percent were foreign born, but many native-born Tejanos reported that one or both parents were immigrants.[29]

Isolation from mainstream institutions strengthened cohesiveness of the immigrant communities. Residential segmentation was the order of the day in Texas, and physical distance prevented Tejanos from interacting with whites to a great degree.[30] Those who lived along the border towns, furthermore, turned to Mexico as an alternative market, regardless of social class. They read Spanish-language newspapers published in Mexico, sent their children to be educated in the motherland, and traveled south for pleasure or to buy fineries and other luxuries.[31]

Rural residence also acted as a historical force that perpetuated insular group characteristics. Close to 75 percent of the Tejano community during this period was rural,[32] laying track for the expanding railroad and performing other undesirable duties but most commonly using agrarian skills and applying them as day laborers on emerging farmlands. As already noted, Texas Mexicans during this era turned to migrant labor, roaming from the farms of the Coastal Bend area of South Texas to those in Far East Texas.[33]

Similarly isolated were the New Mexican pastores who moved into the Panhandle with their sheep in the late 1870s. Originally, these pastores had come with a New Mexican of prominence named Casimero Romero and established homes in the Canadian River Valley; they brought with them household needs and ranch gear and some forty-five hundred head of sheep, numerous horses, and a plentiful supply of livestock to furnish them with meat and milk. Other sheepmen followed, seeking to take advantage of the free range in the Panhandle's unsettled plains. Prosperity followed; the ranchmen marketed their wool in Las Vegas, New Mexico, and as far away as Dodge City, Kansas. But then in the early 1880s, a series of freezing winters devastated the sheep herds. More ominously, Anglo cattlemen who had moved into the region almost simultaneously began acquiring titles to much of the land that the sheepmen had claimed for years. As they "legitimized" their claims, the ranchers drove out the sheepmen, thus snuffing out the short life of these early Mexican-American settlements in the Texas Panhandle (1874–1884).[34]

Concentration in menial occupations also produced Tejano detachment from Anglo society, thereby further nourishing immigrant cultural forms. The economic changes that took Texas in dramatic new directions in the last half of the nineteenth century allowed some Tejanos to find opportunity in white-collar positions and the professions, but their numbers remained modest. As of the turn of the century, 54.5 percent of the Tejano population was concentrated in the sector of the economy classified by the Census Bureau as "unspecialized labor."[35]

Government neglect of the Tejano population may be identified as one more factor that helped to preserve immigrant expressions. Until the 1880s, politicians pursued a laissez-faire attitude toward societal problems in general, but even when progressive reformers undertook efforts to improve education, prison life, and the condition of eleemosynary institutions in the early twentieth century, they did not consciously direct their efforts at Texas Mexicans. Indeed, little existed in Texas comparable to efforts in the Northeastern United States where educators used the public schools as institutions to acculturate the children of immigrants. To the contrary, the education of Tejanitos remained a remote concern to white society, since some believed in keeping an uneducated proletariat, or, at best, providing Tejanos only the fundamentals of learning.

Actually, elements within the Tejano community rejected the acculturation of the young into the dominant society. While some Tejanos of means did send their children to private Catholic schools and American colleges, others enrolled their children in private schools with curriculums emphasizing the values and heritage of Mexico. One such institution was established near Ysleta in 1871, while the popular Aoy School (a Mexican Preparatory School) started in El Paso in 1887. In the 1890s, Mexican-American residents of Hebbronville founded the Colegio Altamirano, and those of Laredo established the Colegio Preparatorio in 1906. The Escuela Particular opened circa 1909 in Zapata County, and another private school started in Laredo in 1911.[36]

THE PLACE OF WOMEN

In their views toward women, Tejanos adhered to a certain ideal that was rooted in Mexican culture, though the Texas frontier experience mitigated that notion. There prevailed, for instance, a double standard of morality. Moral codes called for women to be chaste at first marriage (mothers cautioned their daughters: *cuida la honra*—guard your honor) and remain faithful to their spouses thereafter, even if their husbands turned into shameless philanderers. In actuality, this behavior was not confined to the Latin temperament, for similar expressions of masculine traits may be found in other western cultures. (As an example of such *machismo*, there existed in Texas during the nineteenth century the so-called paramour statute which permitted a man to kill his wife's lover without fear of legal retribution.)[37]

The Mexican male in the ideal dictated that his daughters and wife remain at home, the latter to raise the children and keep the household. And women themselves may have preferred this domestic role—such a desire was not out of the ordinary, however, for in this sense Tejanas resembled other nineteenth-century women who held similar preferences.[38] But in reality, Tejano society overlooked such scriptures. For one thing, women were compelled to seek employment outside the home in order to subsidize the family income. Statistics bear out the violation of cultural restraints. In 1850, working women partly supported some 5.2 percent of Tejano households, but that figure had increased almost fourfold by 1900.[39]

In fact, Tejanas themselves skirted the maxim that they ought to be homebound. There are the cases of Mexican-born women such as Sara Estela Ramírez and Santa Teresa Urrea, for example, who assumed activist roles, though in different callings. Ramírez in 1901 joined Ricardo Flores Magón, who arrived in Laredo in 1904 to establish the main offices for the *Partido Liberal Mexicano* (PLM). The PLM sought the overthrow of Mexican president Porfirio Diáz, the achievement of a broad transformation in Mexico's institutions, but also the organization of Texas-Mexican laborers throughout the various Mexican-American communities in Texas. From 1904 until the time of her death in 1910, Ramírez took part in labor activity in the border area, but additionally, she established a reputation as an accomplished author of poems, essays, and other literary articles.[40]

Urrea, on the other hand, was a *curandera* (folk healer) who came to El Paso in 1896, fleeing political opponents who charged her with participation in the efforts to incite a popular rebellion against Diáz. During her brief stay in the city, Santa Teresa reportedly healed numerous patients.[41]

TIES TO THE HOMELAND

Curanderos in Mexican society were thought capable of effecting cures through special healing powers. During this period, additionally, folk healers stood as crucial symbols linking Texas Mexicans to the traditional past in a world in rapid flux, according to the anthropologist/folklorist José E. Limón. This is evident in the career of Guadalajara-born Don Pedrito Jaramillo, who practiced curanderismo in South Texas from 1881 until his death in 1907. As Texas society changed in the late nineteenth and early twentieth centuries, Don Pedrito came to symbolize a bulwark against the social transformation. His shrine at Los Olmos (near present-day Falfurrias in Brooks County) provided a sanctuary where Tejanos could identify with the values of the old culture at a time when an emphasis on progress and material advancement subverted the foundations of the familiar pastoral society.[42]

Corridos were important ethnic instruments by which people gave account of individual or community sentiments. Epic events, for example, could be narrated through the corridos, and the subjects of the adventure could be either glorified or disparaged. This was the case of *"El corrido de José Mosqueda"* which told of the Mosqueda gang's robbery of the Rio Grande Railroad on January 1, 1891, between Port Isabel and Brownsville. In the 1890s, the ballad related the grief of those victimized by the theft, the anxiety of the men implicated in the crime, and both support for and disgust with the perpetrators who fled across the Rio Grande with part of the plunder.[43]

Border ballads further tell of Tejano discontent with social relations and display the bitterness felt toward the Anglo authority structure. One corrido extolled the exploits of Jacinto Treviño who in July 1910 took on the Texas Rangers after killing a white man who had beaten his younger brother to death. When the Rangers set up an ambush for Treviño near San Benito, he outwitted them, waylaying the officers instead, and killed or injured four of the rangers before fleeing to Mexico. Treviño became a wanted man but a hero within the Tejano community for his bravery in taking on the hated rinches. In 1971, a college in Mercedes (in the Lower Rio Grande Valley) was named after him, though the school did not thrive.[44]

Corridos could also be employed as a cultural expression of disapproval of the rapidly changing times, a theme Professor Limón detects in the ballad *"El corrido de Gregorio Cortéz."* As mentioned earlier in this chapter, Cortéz had shot a peace officer in Karnes County, and, fearing for his life, he cut across the South Texas countryside towards Laredo. While white society saw Cortéz as a murderer, Texas Mexicans sympathized with the fugitive and assisted his flight to the border by providing him with horses, ammunition, and food. Finally captured after ten days of running, he was tried and convicted for the killing of a member of the pursuing posse (the governor pardoned him from prison in 1913).

Countless corridos immortalized Cortéz and his escapade with the Anglos. According to Limón, the ballad narrative of Cortéz's heroism and epic struggle helped Texas Mexicans identify with an earlier time, before the economic changes of the early twentieth century had deteriorated the quality of their lives. For Tejanos, Cortéz represented the time during which they had lorded over the range lands as skillful horsemen.[45]

Ties to the homeland are also evident in political interaction with Mexico. Tejanos stayed abreast of Mexican politics through family ties or through first-hand information provided by migrants entering Texas to engage in seasonal labor. On the other hand, many immigrants made Texas their home not only because of improved economic prospects but because they had chosen exile in the state to escape the economic and political tyranny of Don Porfirio.

The Texas-Mexican community thus supported Catarino Garza's liberal politics (disseminated through Garza's South Texas newspapers *El Libre Pensador* and *El Comercio Mexicano*) denouncing the Mexican president's stranglehold on the executive.[46] In 1891, Garza (whose attempted murder had led to the aforementioned Rio Grande City riot of 1888) and his army of volunteers set out from Starr County, determined to stir popular upheaval against the dictator. But American troops intervened upon Mexican soil to halt the assault, and Garza retreated to Texas to plan future attacks from Duval County and the border region, though little ever materialized. American officials moved in to remove Garza and his conspirators but found the population of South Texas uncooperative, shielding the revolutionary instead.[47] Ultimately, he made his way to Houston, New Orleans, and Key West, Florida, where he and his brother became involved in the revolutionary activities of Cuban exiles. He met his death as a filibusterer in Colombia in 1895.[48]

Tejanos in a Multicultural Society

Though Anglo Americans by the 1880s controlled practically every mainstream institution affecting Tejanos, and though the economic transformation of the era had impacted adversely upon Texas-Mexican workers, Mexican Americans showed resiliency in adapting to modernity. Tejano entrepreneurs sought to penetrate new business opportunities, civic activists attempted to carve greater roles for themselves in politics, and laborers tried to help themselves and their fellow workers through contacts with United States labor unions that were organizing in Texas.

Such efforts at acculturation were undertaken even as Tejanos affirmed their own group identity. Some went about their lives as unreconstructed nationalists stern in their fidelity to Mexican tradition. Many others sought to mold their destiny as part of a syncretic culture: two heritages, two world views. This latter element, diverse in the gradation of acculturation, occupied an uncommon place in Texas society, able to move to varying degrees between the cultural polarity of the recent arrivals from Mexico and that of the Americanized, chauvinistic Texan.

CHAPTER FIVE

Corridors North
1900–1930

FROM the 1890s and continuing until the beginning of the Great Depression, an estimated 1.5 million people found their way from Mexico to the United States.[1] For a brief time, the immigrants who arrived in Texas tugged at the sentiments of residents of urban *colonias* (Mexican-American settlements) and rural hamlets—using the old country as a point of moral and spiritual reference. Natives and even nonnatives, however, looked no further than their country of residence—the United States—for their identity. This dichotomy—wherein an immigrant and a Mexican-American ethnicity coexisted, even competed with one another—stands as a unique phenomenon in Tejano (and therefore Mexican-American) history.[2] Consequently, the immigrant experience and the Americanization process that unfolded during this era receive equal space in this book, in Chapters Five and Six, respectively.

A New Migratory Wave

PUSH AND PULL FACTORS

What caused this unprecedented transborder migration? Students of immigration break down the explanation into push and pull factors. Compelling people to leave Mexico for the United States in the latter years of the nineteenth century and extending into 1910 were the distressful conditions many faced under the dictatorship of President Porfirio Diáz. The rural poor were forcibly removed from their common lands by ambitious land barons and faced a dismal life of peonage on the rural estates. Population increases in the late nineteenth century, moreover, weighed on Mexico's semifeudal subsistence economy, compelling the peasantry to search elsewhere for opportunity, often in the United States.[3]

The Mexican Revolution which broke out in 1910 and lasted until 1920 also became a catalyst for migration. Mexicans fled to the United States to escape the horrors of war or reprisals from the feuding factions. Even after the fighting had ended, life during Mexico's reconstruction in the 1920s was still precarious, for armed rebels still roamed the land, food shortages plagued the population, and unemployment ran amok.

By the 1920s, on the other hand, an economic revolution unfolding along the United States border enticed thousands to leave their struggling country to try their luck in a more peaceful land. From the 1880s to the early 1900s, thousands of miles of railroad rails were laid to connect the American Southwest to the United States economy. Mining companies began the exploitation of copper and coal. Farmers in the Lower Rio Grande Valley transformed old ranchos, which they had recently acquired, into profitable citrus and cotton concerns. Increasingly, railroad contractors, mining companies, and agriculturists in Texas and other parts of the United States looked south to Mexico as a source of needed labor.

The United States' involvement in World War I created further labor scarcities. The Immigration Act of 1917 had closed the door on European laborers wishing to immigrate. Then millions of American workers flocked to new factories or went off to do their patriotic chore.[4]

The economic boom of the 1920s served to maintain the influx of Mexicans into Texas of the previous two decades. Large-scale growers, especially, welcomed the immigrants, claiming them to have a specific suitability for stoop work. Actually, such attitudes justified efforts at exploitation. Congressman John Nance Garner of Uvalde rationalized it thusly in 1920 while testifying before the House Immigration and Naturalization Committee, arguing in favor of a more open U.S.-Mexico border:

I believe I am within the bounds of truth when I say that the Mexican man is a superior laborer when it comes to grubbing land. . . . And I may add that the prices that they charge are much less than the same labor would be from either the negro or the white man and for the same time they do . . . a third more—they produce a third more results from their labor than either the negro or white man would do.[5]

So much did growers wish to rely on Mexican hands that a profitable business of smuggling immigrants into Texas fields developed despite statutes forbidding recruiters from contracting labor in foreign nations. Labor agents crossed the border into Mexico and, with promises of higher wages, smuggled workers across the Rio Grande and shipped them to different destinations.[6]

HOW MANY IMMIGRANTS?

Demographers find it difficult to ascertain how many people crossed from Mexico into the Texas and the rest of the United States. In the period before the 1920s, there existed a more or less unpoliced U.S.-Mexican border. The United States Department of Labor established the Border Patrol in 1924, but its time was taken up by the enforcement of customs laws and Prohibition. The government imposed certain stipulations for entering into the United States in 1924, some of which involved entry fees which the Mexican immigrants could ill afford. While some immigrants entered legally, many avoided bureaucratic entanglements. Thus, precision in calculating the number of Mexican immigrants that came to Texas is imprecise,[7] but according to the best estimates the figures for the "Mexico-born population," 1900–1930 were:

1900	1910	1920	1930
71,062	125,016	251,827	266,364[8]

RESTRICTIONIST DEBATE

Americans divided on the merits of permitting a dramatic increase in immigration from Mexico. Warnings regarding the dangers of too many Mexicans in the United States had actually been sounded in the early twentieth century, but nativism escalated by the 1920s. The debate over immigration took two paths. Advocates of an open border insisted that the matter was a harmless one. Restrictionists, on the other hand, saw many perils in a Mexican immigration floodtide.[9]

The debate turned on both economic and racial convictions. The antirestrictionists advanced the economic argument that U.S. agriculture could not survive if government interrupted immigration. Growers maintained that immigrants worked hard and did not demand the high wages wanted by Anglos. Antirestrictionists also tried to assure those fearing social ruination that the "Mexican Problem" was manageable. They conceded that Mexicans were a degenerate people and posed some moral and political dangers to the country, but advocates of unobstructed migration argued that Mexicans were, all in all, docile and law-abiding and insisted that their presence could be controlled by restricting their employment opportunities to the fields where they would not jeopardize the fabric of white society.[10]

Small-scale farmers and Anglo field hands, conversely, challenged the notion of free admittance into the country, for immigrants were willing to work for less and kept American cotton pickers from making honest wages. Labor unions also sought to arrest easy entry into the country, fearing that Mexican immigrants might, once across the border, reject farm work and seek employment in industrial capacities. A cast of politicians, educators, concerned citizens, and racists further argued that racially backward Mexicans disrupted the American way of life and caused disease, crime, and various other problems.[11]

By the end of the 1920s, the restrictionists triumphed over the antirestrictionists as the United States government directed consuls to exercise greater controls in granting passports to Mexicans. Though the number of entrance visas granted to Mexicans fell after 1929, by then the depression had begun to hamper immigration northward from Mexico.[12]

DISPERSAL

Many of the Mexican immigrants who came to the United States between 1900 and 1930 arrived in the border towns such as El Paso and Laredo by train, for railways by the latter part of the nineteenth century connected numerous points in Mexico to Texas. From these settlements on the Rio Grande, and San Antonio in the interior, the immigrants dispersed into all parts of the state,[13] even penetrating those sections only lightly pioneered by the Texas Mexicans during the nineteenth century.

The areas most heavily impacted by immigration, expectedly, were the older Tejano strongholds of the trans-Nueces and the El Paso and San Antonio regions. South Texas attracted Mexican nationals because it was not far away and because farming in the Rio Grande Valley offered much opportunity picking cotton, vegetables, and some fruits. In Nueces County, where the economic transformation from ranch to cotton farm unfolded between 1900 and 1910, the immigrants worked crops on lands that they had recently grubbed of brush.[14]

The El Paso Valley and the newer West Texas region similarly saw tremendous expansion in their foreign-born Tejano populations. "El Paso symbolized to Mexicans what New York had represented to European immigrants: the opening to what they believed would be a better life," explains the historian Mario T. García. From the 1880s until the early decades of the twentieth century, this border town and its environs offered employment for down-and-out Mexican workers as it became a booming metropolis (El Paso's population increased from 39,571 in 1920 to 58,291 in 1930) and the valley around it developed into a thriving cotton-farming section.[15] At the same time, small, emerging settlements in West Texas needed a great influx of range hands to handle sheep and cattle as well as field workers for new cotton-farming operations.[16]

San Antonio lured its share of immigrants owing to its proximity to the border but also because burgeoning businesses needed unskilled workers. Immigrants, furthermore, saw it as a good home quarters for seasonal migration. Between 1900 and 1930, therefore, the Alamo City's Mexican population increased from 13,722 to 82,373, a substantial percentage of this number claiming foreign birth.[17] From Béxar, Mexicans sojourned north or to nearby farms (where some became sharecroppers alongside African-American and Anglo renters). San Antonio, noted one observer, "poured out Mexicans into the cotton fields with such speed that by 1920, the greatest density of rural Mexican population in Texas was not along the Rio Grande but in Caldwell County in sight of the dome of the State Capitol." By 1930, several counties around the cities of Austin and Waco contained fledgling Mexican enclaves.[18]

Mexicans were not only entering new geographic locales during this period but also habitats that lacked the old Hispanic ambient that existed in South Texas and the Béxar region. These new places, furthermore, contained overwhelming white and black majorities. Certainly, such descriptions applied to East and North Texas, which also received Mexican immigrants. Work in *el traque* (railroad tracks) lured many to Houston by the 1910s, for instance, but the Bayou City's incredible rise as a major oil and gas production center opened many other sorts of employment for immigrants as did the Houston Ship Channel, the cotton compresses, the textile mills, and construction companies. By 1910, some two thousand Mexicans had settled in Houston since the 1880s and 1890s. Twenty years later, the city's Mexican-origin population stood at 15,000, many of them immigrants. Mexicans could also be found in Beaumont and Galveston by the 1910s.[19]

In North Texas, the Dallas–Fort Worth area saw the beginnings of Mexican settlements similar to those in Houston. By the 1910s, immigrants fleeing the Mexican Revolution mixed with Tejano day laborers working with local railroad companies and founded a barrio just north of Dallas's central business district, there joined by others doing pick-and-shovel work on gas and sewer systems, streets, and street-car lines. In the 1930s the U.S. Census counted nearly 6000 persons of Mexican descent in Dallas, many of whom had made their way north from Mexico and lived in barrios with such names as "Indiana Alley" and "Los Altos de Juárez."[20] In Fort Worth, the Mexican population stood at 4,426 in 1920, but declined to 3,955 ten years later.[21] Like San Antonio in Central Texas, Dallas and Fort Worth turned out Mexicans into neighboring cotton counties, among them Ellis and Kaufman.

But immigrants found other places in North Texas offering employment, such as Milam County where they worked on farms and in lignite mines, in Robertson County where some became wood choppers, and in Denton County where they turned to farm, ranch, or railroad jobs. As of 1930, however, the number of Tejanos in North Texas in no way compared to figures in the southern and far western regions of the state.[22]

The Immigrant Generation

For the most part, those who came to Texas from Mexico descended from the class of poor folks. These economic refugees were the ones to cause the aforementioned dilemma of the 1920s: they worked cheaply and performed labor shunned by whites, yet were seen as a social danger to the country because of their alleged illiteracy, propensity to commit crime and cause disease, and reluctance to acculturate.

An upper class of *ricos* (wealthy people) and a middle class of professionals also fled northward, hoping to stay in Texas temporarily until politics stabilized in Mexico. These included exiles whose ties to the Porfirian order made their stay precarious in Mexico; others were landowners trekking to Texas to escape the wrath of vindictive peasant armies. In the 1920s, the political emigrés were followed by refugees escaping the turmoil in Mexico created by the anti-Catholic administration of President Plutarco Elías Calles. Though not as significant in size compared to the bulk of those who descended from the lower class, the ricos could be influential due to their backgrounds as people of education and means. These families were to be found in the Lower Rio Grande Valley, San Antonio, Laredo, El Paso, and Houston.[23]

In Texas this corps of elites played significant roles in ethnic enclaves. They promoted a Mexican past through the distribution of Mexican books, magazines, musical records, and Spanish-language newspapers from Mexico City. They sponsored speaking engagements and theatrical performances and editorialized or extolled the virtues of *la patria* (Mexico, their native country). Meantime, they formed their own clubs and held exclusive cultural activities. They maintained a commitment to preserving Mexican nationalist sentiments within the community of immigrants.[24]

IMPLANTATION

Many of the immigrants had planned to stay in Texas only long enough to make enough money to permit them to live a more comfortable life back in the homeland. Consequently, they did not pursue American citizenship. In their view, Americans in Mexico were not any more inclined to naturalize, even as they benefitted immensely from the natural resources (such as oil) of that nation. Moreover, many felt Mexico a better country, especially in cultural terms, than the United States. Since they had every intention of returning to the old country, the visitors asked why they should be expected to become citizens.[25]

Thus, in the period from the early twentieth century until the Great Depression, numerous Tejano communities throughout Texas took on a "foreign" quality. Recent arrivals integrated themselves into the local Spanish-surnamed population, renting or building shacks in the Mexican section of town or finding work with Texas-Mexican crews, spending part of their wages in *cantinas* (bars) in the barrio, frequenting Mexican-American gatherings, and even courting the daughters of Texas-born Mexicans.[26] Together, this mass of laboring poor and the *rico* exiles came to constitute what historians refer to as the "Immigrant Generation."[27]

A NONNATIVE WAY

The look to Mexico is discernible in the persistent attachment of the foreign-born to traditional cultural conventions. Detectable in Texas were concepts from south of the Rio Grande that dealt with family cohesion, the roles of males and females, the custom of marriage by late adolescence, and the adherence to Catholicism and the Spanish language. Reinforcing the above understandings were corridos and other songs, poems, folklore and other oral traditions, and Mexican-style ceremonies and social gatherings that were occasioned by weddings, funerals, and religious holy days.[28]

Within such a context, immigrant women did not fare too well. Immigrant males, like Texas-born Mexican-American men, still held the attitude that women's duties consisted of raising children and keeping house, but financial need at times still compelled women to find employment. Wives widowed by the revolution in Mexico now became the sole supporters of the family. The jobs they took, however, were hardly profitable: most took "women's work" and became laundresses or servants in the border cities.[29] To be sure, middle-class women fared better. They enjoyed an improved standard of living and joined exclusive clubs, especially charitable organizations designed to assist the less fortunate members of the colonia.[30]

In the more rural areas, life may have been more restrictive. Male heads of families discouraged women from attending school or learning English, as some felt education to be disruptive to male-female relationships. Wives and daughters stayed back on the farm when fathers and sons went into town. Once married, preferably early, wives bore babies successively; most lacked knowledge of birth-control measures, but men also preferred large families, considering a succession of offspring to be a mark of their virility and recognizing the economic benefits to having many children. An older family member, such as a grandmother, or a *partera* (midwife), helped deliver babies at home.[31]

Habitually, the immigrants also used Mexico as a compass for proper behavior. Journalists advised parents, for example, to teach children the ways of propriety, to be sure that they abide by United States laws, and to instill in them racial pride. Cultural and recreative clubs emphasized the need for the preservation of Mexico's good name, as well as its customs and traditions. Fiestas patrias celebrations, which went back to the 1820s in Texas, became yearly rituals for the display of allegiance.[32] Various kinds of entertainment nurtured "*méxico de afuera*" (Mexico in the United States). Theatrical presentations were provided by companies relocated to Texas because of the Mexican Revolution, and the music popular in northern Mexico (such as the accordion-led ensemble called the *conjunto*) was diffused by the newcomers throughout Texas.[33] The Immigrant Generation proclaimed the concept of "Mexican" proudly and patriotically upheld the honor of the homeland.

Conversely, many of the recent immigrants held denigrating views toward the United States and even Mexican Americans, for despite their American pretensions, white society continued to treat them as second-class citizens. Recent immigrants singled out the women, criticizing them for mimicking American customs and fashions. The newcomers referred critically to Tejanos adopting American habits as *pochos*.[34]

LOYALTY AND THE LAND OF BIRTH

The foreign born did not sever their loyalties to the old country either, and in many cities Tejanos maintained connections to specific areas in Mexico, often their hometowns. Some colonias formed associations to raise funds for the relief of victims of natural disasters in Mexico, or for other worthwhile projects in the old country, as when in 1921, the San Antonio community undertook a fundraiser to subsidize the construction of two public schools in Guanajuato. Other drives could involve unique projects. In 1919, people of San Antonio heeded a local call for monies so that the old country could purchase a merchant vessel.[35]

But immigrants also engaged in causes of greater magnitude. The immigrant community included a contingent of political exiles who used Texas as a plotting ground. Also, poor laborers regularly crossed the Rio Grande as part of their migratory pattern of labor and saw their country's despair first hand. Further, family ties to people affected by the tyranny of Don Porfirio and the Mexican Revolution after 1910 motivated the refugees to support one cause or another. In Houston, for instance, the refugee community established *La Sociedad Mexicana "Vigilancia"* in 1914 to aid the forces of Venustiano Carranza, who led a movement to remove the Díaz surrogate Victoriano Huerta.[36]

The most prominent case of revolutionary activity in Texas against Don Porfirio involved the aforementioned Ricardo Flores Magón and his PLM. Magón's PLM intrigued to remove the Mexican dictator in the hope of implementing significant changes that would, among other things, bring relief to the lower classes through land reform and prolabor policies.[37] PLM newspapers in the years before the Mexican Revolution were located in San Antonio, Del Rio, and El Paso[38], and through *Regeneración*, the PLM's primary journalistic organ, Magón appealed to Tejano workers who identified with their comrades in the homeland or were dissatisfied with job conditions in the state. Though it is difficult to measure the ideological impact of the PLM, the party had followers as deep as Central Texas. The PLM local *"Tierra y Libertad"* of Austin, for instance, organized an impressive rally at Uhland, Texas, on Labor Day of 1912, and roughly one thousand people from other PLM chapters in Central Texas attended. After inspirational speeches that urged societal changes in Mexico and the United States, delegates dispersed to campaign in their own communities for the goals of the PLM.[39] In actuality, immigrants in the early twentieth century stayed out of movements that appeared to be radical for fear of jeopardizing their work or risking extradition, though some did participate in the labor struggles of the era.[40]

The PLM also exhorted women to join its ranks and fight on behalf of workers and women's emancipation. Indeed, women members of the PLM participated as speakers and fundraisers in forums and rallies held in El Paso, Brownsville, and Zapata and Frio counties on the eve of the Mexican Revolution. Among the PLM's several women activists was Sara Estela Ramírez, mentioned in the previous chapter.[41]

By no means was the PLM alone in work related to political developments in Mexico. There was, for example, *La Grán Liga Mexicana*, formed in 1909, which, in contrast to the PLM, favored Díaz and collaborated with local workers' organizations in San Antonio to try to help the dictator continue his prolandholder and probusiness government.[42]

SELF-HELP SOCIETIES

Mutual aid societies first appeared among Texas-Mexicans in the 1870s, but they proliferated with the coming of the Immigrant Generation and by the 1920s could be found in most regions of the state including the Big Bend and North Texas. Such organizations grew out, in part, from the circumstances many Tejanos experienced regularly before white society: public humiliation, violence, and poverty, to list only the most salient afflictions. Despite the cause for their origins, mutualist societies tended to be nonconfrontational, concentrating instead on improving conditions for their members and other working-class people through intellectual and spiritual stimulation, social camaraderie, and through creating a congenial and familiar environment in an adopted world.[43]

Several characteristics marked these societies as a product of the immigrant's temperament, though membership usually included U.S. Mexicans. Generally, the societies carried the name of a national hero from Mexico such as Benito Juárez. Members preferred to use Spanish when conducting business. Organizers emphasized Mexican ideals and values and held reservations about assimilation and integration into a racist society, though they were not opposed to joining the mainstream on an equal basis.[44] While these benefit societies maintained a regard for the affairs of Mexico, and sometimes donated to worthy causes for the old country, their primary concern was the welfare of their community and the well-being of their families in particular.[45]

Because of such concerns, obreros founded mutualista labor associations. Shunned by the American Federation of Labor (which had, as mentioned, made some gestures towards incorporating Mexicans, though it began to look upon them as strikebreakers) and Mexican consuls who feared alienating the United States government, immigrant laborers turned to models used in Mexico wherein craftsmen were organized into mutualistas. In San Antonio, for instance, bakers founded the *Sociedad Morelos Mutua de Panaderos* which struck for decent wages and working conditions in 1917.[46]

Women participated in mutualistas as officers and committee heads and even founders. For example, María L. Hernández and her husband Pedro of San Antonio, Texas, organized the *Orden Caballeros de America* in 1929 to help solve educational problems for Tejanos and to promote civic and political activism beneficial to Mexicans, whether native or foreign-born.[47] Still, students of mutualistas disagree on the roles women played in these associations. Like men, some joined for self-protection and probably did not advocate a feminist agenda. However, some of the middle-class participants did assail the double standard and urged women in general to take stands against the consumption of alcohol, war, and the subordination of women.[48]

THE IMMIGRANT PRESS

Spanish language newspapers, often owned by political refugees and read by thousands of new arrivals (not to mention native-born Texas Mexicans) served as vehicles that steadied the Mexican connection. These presses praised Mexico and its people and denounced white Americans for inflicting abuses upon immigrants and Mexican Americans. They devoted extensive and continuous coverage to national causes in the old country.[49] Additionally, these newspapers stressed the need to preserve the old way of life, published creative pieces of literature, praised musical artists and theatrical companies performing in nearby towns, and gave much coverage to religious and secular celebrations in the community.[50] Simultaneously, they critiqued those practices that appeared incompatible with the sense of social justice proclaimed by Americans.

Among the most widely read was *La Prensa* of San Antonio, established by Ignacio E. Lozano in 1913. A daily distributed throughout many parts of the United States and the northern states of Mexico, *La Prensa* had as its audience the refugees, especially the rico class, and consequently denounced the string of revolutionary governments that took power in Mexico during the 1910s and 1920s. Though Lozano's elitist politics hardly harmonized with the sentiments of the many poor refugees, his efforts did influence the manner of political sentiments in Texas, for *La Prensa* disseminated the thoughts of Mexico's most prominent intellectuals during the 1910s and 1920s, among them José Vasconcelos.[51]

Summary

In the early decades of the twentieth century waves of immigrants from Mexico invigorated native Texas-Mexican urban and rural settlements and even metamorphosed some of them into largely immigrant communities.[52] In Mexican enclaves resided an array of groups differing in class, status, and political visions, with numerous clubs, newspapers, labor associations, churches, and other institutions vying to meet their diverse expectations.

The presence of such large numbers of foreigners modified, albeit temporarily, the nineteenth-century adaptation of Mexicans to Texas. Briefly, a Mexican "presence" vied for ascendancy in the Tejano community with an American "presence." This struggle would last no more than a generation, for the sentiments of many born in the United States, or others taking a liking to its institutions, would increasingly turn to the country of their birth or adoption, not Mexico.[53]

CHAPTER SIX

The World War One Years and the 1920s

DURING the nineteen-year span between 1910 and 1930, Texas entered an age of modernity. The transition did not exactly improve the quality of life for the majority of Texans of Mexican descent (Roberto M. Villarreal estimates their numbers at some 695,000 for 1930),[1] however: in many cases, in fact, the arrival of the new age only exacerbated a bad condition.

Tejano Life in the Modern Age

ON THE FARMS

By the early decades of the twentieth century, cotton had already established its reign as king in Texas. Along the border in South Texas, farmers arrived from states in the Midwest and North, and by the 1910s they had ushered in a veritable farm revolution (this influx of Anglos diluted the Mexican population advantage throughout South Texas).[2] Central Texas farms continued to harvest the old staple; in Central Texas, tenant farming and sharecropping had become a fact of life for numerous poor whites, African Americans, and even recently arrived Tejano workers. The region of West Texas beyond the 100th meridian had also embraced the switch to cotton, and even the El Paso Valley, situated in one of the most arid regions of the United States, had yielded to cotton growing by the 1910s, primarily along a stretch of fertile land parallel to the Rio Grande east of El Paso.[3]

This transformation in the rural sector affected Tejanos in several ways. Economically, it shocked the landed aristocracy of South Texas, as the newly arrived Anglo farmers displaced more of the old rancheros through forced sales, strong-arm tactics, and legal acquisitions when Tejanos faced uncertainty due to taxes, unpaid loans, and an unpredictable market for their livestock. More fortunate were Tejano counterparts in predominantly ranch counties such as Webb, Zapata, Kenedy, Brooks, and Jim Hogg where the topography encouraged livestock raising instead of crops. Also able to weather the Anglo farmers' encroachment were some of the Tejano stockmen in Duval and Starr counties who had switched effectively to careers in agricultural husbandry.[4]

For common folks, the cotton-based agricultural order produced newer labor situations. By the 1920s, the majority of Tejano farm workers made their living in one of two ways: as various types of sharecroppers or, most commonly, as migrant seasonal workers on commercial farms.[5] Tejanos picked cotton in South and Central Texas (in 1910, for wages of 50 cents per hundred pounds; this increased to $1.00 after World War I)[6] but began heading *"pal wes"* (*para el west*, or to West Texas) where the new farms lured them in unprecedented numbers. By the 1920s, Tejanos traveling in family units were staying after the cotton-picking season and taking up residence in towns such as Sweetwater, Lamesa, Rotan, Tahoka, Littlefield, Muleshoe, Lubbock, and Plainview. In this early period, however, most remained migrants and returned to South or Central Texas.

The agricultural transformation of the age also affected Tejanos politically, especially in the rural communities of South Texas where the new Anglo farmers, through reform groups and alliances, sought to dislodge the old Tejano Democratic bosses. The recent arrivals worked specifically to deprive Mexicans of the vote, through the establishment of poll taxes (which many Tejanos could not afford) or the new practice adopted by the White Man's Primary Association that required those wishing to vote in primary elections to go before a committee and declare, "I am a white person and a Democrat." By the late 1910s, much of the Mexican-American population in the farm counties of South Texas had been disfranchised through whites-only primaries, threats of firings from their jobs or of bodily harm, and various methods that might include not informing Tejanos about scheduled elections. Excep-

PANHAND

Amarillo

Hereford

South Pla

Muleshoe
Plainview

Littlefield

Lubbock

Tahoka

W E S T

Lamesa

Ro

Sv

NEW MEXICO

Garden
City

El Paso
Ysleto
Socorro
San Elizario

FAR

Pecos

T E X A

S
An

WEST

Fort
Stockton

River

TEXAS

Alpine

Rocks

Rio

Grande

De

MEXICO

0 miles   100   200   300

0 kilometers 100   200   300

Twentieth Century
Texas

OKLAHOMA

Red River

ARKANSAS

Cross Timbers

Thurber

Dallas

Fort Worth

Piney

Sabine

Woods

Nacogdoches

Sabine River

Brazos River

Waco

LOUISIANA

orado

Trinity River

Thorndale

Austin

River

Kyle

Bastrop

Beaumont

San Marcos

Lockhart

New Braunfels

Houston

ountry

an Antonio

CENTRAL

Wharton

stroville

Ganado

Galveston

Pearsall T E X A S

Victoria

Edna

tal

Kenedy

Winter

Three

Golaid

Cotulla

Rivers

R.

Beeville

os

Nueces

Corpus

Christi

Coastal Bend

Robstown

aredo

San Diego

Alice

Driscoll

Nuevo

Laredo

Kingsville

Hebbronville

Falfarrias

Gulf of Mexico

e

Roma

Rio Grande City

Edinburg

Edcouch Elsa

Grande

San Benito

alley

Mission

San Juan

Mercedes

Port Isabel

Brownsville

tion again must be made of the ranch counties of the region, where Mexican officeholders remained active in politics.[7]

IN THE TOWNS

For many Tejanos living in cities, livelihood depended on occupations that were not a significant improvement over wage labor on the expanding farms (as noted, Mexican migrant workers used urban sites by the 1920s as home bases for their migration). Poverty for urban Tejanos was still as much a reality at the time of modernity as it had been in the nineteenth century. Old, dilapidated housing, rough and dusty roads, and the lack of sanitary facilities typified El Paso's south side, San Antonio's West Side, and Houston's budding east side. Malnutrition and disease plagued the barrios of the state's municipalities. Barrio residents faced extremely high rates of infant mortality, tuberculosis, and other maladies.[8]

The Mexican sections continued to be separate enclaves within the state's cities. While no legal restrictions outwardly prohibited Mexicans from living in the better homes in better neighborhoods, racial segregation persisted due to a combination of poverty, a preference many Tejanos had for living in an in-group environment, and the strengthening of Jim Crow laws and attitudes, for values in the cities often chimed with those in the state's rural areas. In the Anglo communities, new and popular notions charging that Mexicans were unhygienic barred Tejanos from admittance to eating establishments, drugstores, barbershops, banks, movie theaters, and miscellaneous public places.[9]

Segregated schools were the rule in most towns, and neither the Texas government nor the general society was particularly committed to educating Texas-Mexican students. Texas farmers were interested in having a readily available supply of field workers, something made more probable by discouraging Mexicans from acquiring an education. Thus, Mexican schools in Texas ordinarily lacked proper facilities or provisions. Furthermore, some towns prohibited Mexicans from advancing further than the sixth grade. According to a survey taken in 1928, some 40 percent of the school-aged Tejano children received no instruction between 1927 and 1928.[10]

While the above experiences applied to the majority of Texas Mexicans in the new age, a middle class still remained. In communities such as El Paso, Brownsville, and Laredo, Texas Mexicans were employed in city or county government, taught in the public schools, and worked as compositors, printers, and salespersons. These cities even had some Tejano doctors and lawyers.[11] Furthermore, new immigrants as well as Mexican Americans continued to operate small-scale enterprises that serviced the Mexican population. In Houston, for instance, a downtown Mexican commercial district included retail stores, barbershops, restaurants, bookstores, doctors' offices, pharmacies, and a theater (Tejano customers even rode the trolley cars into the district from their homes).[12]

SHIFTING LOYALTIES

Diverse ideological and philosophical expressions emanated from the Tejano community during this epoch. Present, of course, was a strain of cultural conduct carried on by those folks with strong links to old Mexico. Also, many Texas-born Mexicans perpetuated the traditional values of their upbringing in colonias and remote rural villages. In their views toward the role of women, for example, Tejanos insisted on adhering to old ways: girls were to be strictly chaperoned when in the company of boys and were to accept their role as exemplary wives, mothers, and homemakers. Some parents looked askance at American customs; to many of them, United States traditions represented disobedience, a loose morality, elopement and an early divorce.[13]

But residence in Texas seduced many Tejanos into embracing the very system that shut them off. Even as Tejanos may have been facing nativism, political disfranchisement, and the old and severe problems such as land loss, lynchings, and scarce economic opportunities, forces of socialization during the era offered enticements that produced a middle course between the world view of the less acculturated masses and the milieu of the Americanized Euro-Texan. Tejanos residing in the cities (some 25 percent lived in metropolitan areas in the 1920s, according to some estimates)[14] came in contact with Americanizing agents, among them mass culture, modern innovations, and ideological currents. They also had contact with mainstream institutions which penetrated even the segregated barrios. By World War I, for example, Mexican theaters showed (in addition to films produced in Mexico) American movies starring Charlie Chaplin and Mary Pickford. Charity and reform groups that could be found in cities such as San Antonio, El Paso, and Houston acted as conduits that Americanized barrio residents by sponsoring classes on health, holding sporting activities, and training teenage girls in numerous American crafts. Parochial schools, furthermore, taught allegiance to the United States and instilled in the students' minds the notion of the American promise. Church social centers and even the Catholic Youth Organization assisted in converting impressionable youngsters.[15]

Public schools also helped to shape Tejanitos' sensibilities, even as school facilities left much to be desired and as Anglo-controlled school districts discouraged attendance. In the classroom, teachers instructed their charges on the need to learn English. This approach would help direct sentiments toward the United States and American principles, thereby helping Tejanos improve themselves in society's mainstream.[16] By the 1920s, moreover, the number of school-age Texas-Mexican students had increased, so that educators prompted state officials to implement curriculum reforms that attended to issues such as Tejano poverty, illiteracy, juvenile delinquency, and disease.[17] Thus by the 1920s, a generation of American-raised-and-educated young Tejanos seemed poised to undertake campaigns for the improvement of Mexican-American society. As Jovita González, a writer and folklorist, put it at the end of the 1920s:

> Young Texas-Mexicans are being trained in American [schools]. Behind them lies a store of traditions of another race, customs of past ages, an innate inherited love and reverence for another country. Ahead of them lies a struggle in which they are to be the champions. It is a struggle for equality and justice before the law, for their full rights as American citizens. They bring with them a broader view, a clearer understanding of the good and bad qualities of both races. They are the converging element of two antagonistic civilizations; they have the blood of one and have acquired the ideals of the other.[18]

WORLD WAR I

During World War I, the United States government and society at large made conscious efforts to co-opt the Mexican-American population into the course of national life. As war-related manpower shortages deepened, federal, state, and local authorities called upon all elements of the Texas-Mexican community to join in the defeat of the Axis forces. Being no friend of Germany and perhaps seeing an opportunity for greater social integration in this unprecedented overture, Tejanos responded ungrudgingly. Spanish-language newspapers, for one, hastened U.S.-born Mexicans to display their patriotism and called on those of foreign origin to provide a sympathetic hand to the country that sheltered them. Editors invoked the courage of Mexican and Aztec heroes in their attempts to inspire the community to rally behind the Allied cause.[19]

While the war effort attracted practically every segment of the Texas-Mexican population, most visibly recruited into mobilization campaigns were members constituting the small middle class. As a group, these individuals played an important part in rallying localities to arms. Newspaper editors helped disseminate information issued by draft boards or other government agencies, and prominent citizens such as Clemente Idar of Laredo acted as intermediaries between Anglo officials and the Mexican community. Additionally, Mexican Americans of the middle class sponsored fundraisers and challenged audiences to make contributions at Liberty and War Savings Stamp gatherings: on more than one occasion, the middle-class businessmen and ranchers of South Texas donated generously to such undertakings.[20]

Texas Mexicans contributed to the war effort not only as civilians but as combatants, though the number of Tejanos who participated in World War I is difficult to ascertain at this time. Many fought in the trenches on the western front and earned a laudable record for valor. One of them, Marcelino Serna, a Mexico-born resident of El Paso, earned Italy's Cross of Merit, France's Croix de Guerre and Military Medal, Britain's Medal of Bravery, the Distinguished Service Cross, and two Purple Hearts. His feat of single-handedly taking twenty-four prisoners probably qualified him for the Congressional Medal of Honor, but, in the estimation of historian Carole E. Christian, "He probably did not receive [the Medal] due to his inability to read and write English."[21]

World War I, then, may be identified as a point of departure in mainstream U.S. society's concern for Tejanos. In an effort to make maximum use of the nation's manpower, federal, state, and community officials launched serious drives to incorporate a wider spectrum of the population, including immigrants and Mexican Americans. Following the war, government no longer looked upon them as stepchildren, and society even came to display greater awareness of the Mexican presence.

Texas Mexicans themselves became optimistic about the prospects for real integration and acceptance, but they would be disappointed in their hopes.[22]

IN THE WORKPLACE

In the era between 1910 and 1930, several things coalesced to spur Tejanos to seek further improvements in the workplace. These included the nativist response to recent immigration from Mexico (for it touched Mexican-descent people regardless of nativity), increased politicization among the Americanized sectors of the population, persistent job discrimination, and even social intercourse with fellow obreros at the barroom, the mutualist hall, or the street corner. Collectively, such factors explain some of the early activism on behalf of the exploited proletariat.

Tejanos pursued various avenues in an attempt to improve situations on the job, according to Emilio Zamora, Jr., a student of Texas-Mexican labor in the early twentieth century. Commonly, Tejanos established independent labor organizations. Among the most prominent of these independent bargaining bodies was *La Agrupación Protectora Mexicana* (Mexican Protective Association) established in San Antonio in 1911. Comprised primarily of farm renters and laborers (all Mexicans, whether native- or foreign-born, qualified to join), La Agrupación sought legal protection for its members whenever they faced Anglo-perpetrated violence or illegal dispossession of their property.[23]

Tejanos also attained coalitions with different unions, even as Anglo labor leaders ordinarily rebuffed Mexican initiatives to participate in the broader nationwide labor movement. Tenants, field hands, and an array of city workers in Central Texas, for example, joined affiliates of the Texas Socialist party such as the Land League of America (1914–1917). Worsening economic conditions, exacerbated by the presence of the new immigrant farm hands who depressed wages, explain Tejano motives for joining socialist organizations, but so does the influence of the revolution in Mexico and of newspapers that offered radical alternatives for dealing with poor working conditions. The number of Tejano workers involved with socialist organizations is difficult to determine, though one contemporary member placed it at about one thousand. It was about 1915 when the Texas Socialist party began to disintegrate due to government suppression and a World-War-I-inspired frenzy against radicalism. Mexican socialist organizing faced a similar fate.[24]

Texas-Mexican craftsmen also joined the Texas State Federation of Labor, the state arm of the American Federation of Labor (AFL). They did so as the AFL, for the first time since World War I, extended a helping hand (to insure influence over all sectors of the labor force), recruiting the Laredoan Clemente Idar to travel the state and organize among Texas Mexicans. Though Idar succeeded in his work to some extent, Tejano obreros generally founded local unions on their own initiative, then sought association with the AFL.[25]

Expectedly, most Texas-Mexican unions (regardless of affiliation) were segregated. In El Paso, two such examples in the 1910s were the International Clerk's Protective Association and the Laundry Workers Union. But cases of labor unions with a mixed ethnic membership do exist, though primarily where Tejanos predominated a particular industry. In that border city, one could find Mexican laborers with membership in the Carpenters' Union, the Painters' Union, the Musicians' Union, the Pressmen's Union, and the Freight Handlers' Union.[26]

At present, it is difficult to determine the extent of strikes and violent confrontation between Tejano laborers and management. The historian Mario T. García notes that El Paso was a setting for labor agitation and that numerous small unions, such as those involving clerks, laundry persons, and city public-works employees, struck for worker's rights during the decade of the 1910s.[27] Other scholars have also identified worker discontent and strike activity in San Antonio during the World War I years, one involving Tejano protest against the contract system used in a local federal building project, the other being the bakers' strike mentioned in the previous chapter.[28] In the North Texas town of Thurber, Mexican members of the United Mine Workers' Union took part in a strike in 1926.[29] Ordinarily, strikes taken up by Tejano workers proved unsuccessful, though some did produce slight gains. Management could always hire scabs, use police power, or deport foreign-born laborers to squelch organizing movements.

COLLECTIVE PROTEST

Besides the Tejanos who took active parts in unions to improve their working situations, there were other Tejanos who participated in protest activity. Tejano activists challenged the stultifying living conditions that have been discussed in previous chapters including continued societal injustices; murdering and lynching of innocent Mexicans still persisted in the 1920s, and courts followed the common custom of foregoing penitentiary time for Anglos accused of killing Mexicans.[30]

One expression of Tejanos' political resolve occurred in the West Texas town of San Angelo in September 1910 when Texas-Mexican parents protested school segregation and the inferior education afforded Tejanitos by demanding either the admission of the Mexican children to the white schools or the location of white and Mexican school buildings on the same grounds. When the school board refused to compromise (on the grounds that integration would demoralize the entire school system), students initiated a boycott. For the next several years (1910–1915), parents sent their children to the local Catholic school and a Mexican Presbyterian Mission school which opened late in 1912. By 1915, however, the boycott had lost its momentum and faltered.[31]

A more expressive act of political assertiveness involved the gathering in Laredo of some four hundred delegates—including representatives of mutualistas, various newspaper publishers and reporters, spokespersons for women's causes, and other Tejano leaders—at the invitation of Nicasio Idar and his son and daughter Clemente and Jovita (editors and writers for *La Crónica*) to discuss inequality and discrimination in a public forum. At the *Primer Congreso Mexicanista* (the first Mexican Congress of Texas), held during the week of September 14–22, 1911, speakers addressed the need for unity and denounced inferior schooling, lynchings, labor exploitation, and land loss among Texas Mexicans. Women participants in the assemblage forcefully presented a plank of issues pertaining to women and also established *La Liga Femenil Mexicanista* (the Mexican Feminine League of Texas) whose purpose was to struggle for recognition of individual rights for all Texas Mexicans and more specifically to advance education for Tejanos. The delegates also created a statewide league, *La Grán Liga Mexicanista* (the Grand Mexican League of Texas), entrusted to carry out the goals of the *congreso* and specifically to monitor the manner in which Texas Mexicans were treated in society. In the end, however, the promise of unity advocated by the conference lost its fervency. Several of the mutualist societies preferred autonomy and did not wish to relinquish authority to an umbrella organization.[32]

The most conspicuous example of Texas-Mexican collective protest outside of mainstream politics occurred during the time of the Mexican Revolution (1910–1920) when turmoil in northern Mexico spilled over into South Texas. Tejanos then joined militia-type units in support of the *Plan de San Diego*. Supposedly written in San Diego, Texas, in Duval County, the plan advocated the elimination of "Yankee tyranny" by the waging of a rebellion in February 1915 and the subsequent founding of a new republic constituted of the states lost by Mexico in the Mexican-American War.[33]

The origins of the plan remain obscure. They have been attributed to German intrigue and to Mexico's President Venustiano Carranza's use of border raids as an instrument to acquire U.S. diplomatic recognition in 1915, and the next year to pressure the U.S. into withdrawing General "Black Jack" Pershing's troops from Mexican soil. But according to revisionist historians, the plan was an outgrowth of the prejudice and disdain held by whites towards Texas Mexicans in the South Texas border region.

Leaders of the movement included Luis de la Rosa and Aniceto Pizaña, both from the lower valley, who recruited freely in northern Mexico and South Texas, where the plan had widespread support. From both sides of the border, they launched guerrilla attacks, at times leading parties numbering as high as one hundred men. Border Mexicans and Tejanos joined the insurrectionists to strike back for past and present injustices: landgrabbing, displacement from the old pastoral society, racially motivated violence, and the contemptuous attitudes of the newly arrived Anglo farmers. They attacked and often destroyed farm and ranch operations, irrigation pumps, and transportation lines.

To stem the disturbances, the Texas government dispatched more Texas Rangers to the border and federal troops intensified their patrol of the area. Meantime, volunteer Anglo groups invoked the tradition of nineteenth-century justice, applying lynch law and perpetrating other outrages against defenseless Texas Mexicans and others thought to be in support of the Plan de San Diego.

The border conflict inflicted untold damage on South Texas. The attacks and counterattacks, which were intense from 1915 to 1917, interrupted the sections's economic development, ruined property, and were responsible for the deaths of hundreds of people and the homelessness of thousands. Still, the plan failed to meet its objectives because of poor coordination on the part of the leaders, violence directed at rank-and-file supporters, the militarization of the border, and, very significantly, President Carranza's decision to stop supporting the raiders. As of late 1916, he was still fighting a civil war in Mexico and could ill afford another military engagement. Failure in a military encounter with

U.S. forces would have toppled his presidency. Thus, he barred the raiders' use of northern Mexico as a base from which to launch their expeditions.[34]

POLITICS

Simultaneously, Tejano political participation through mainstream channels reached a low ebb. As noted, political representation at the regional and community levels in the El Paso Valley and in the trans-Nueces may have increased in the later nineteenth and early twentieth centuries, but a decline in the number of Tejano office-holders and involvement in grass-roots decision-making followed in the 1910s and 1920s, save for such ranch counties as Zapata, Duval, Webb and Starr.[35] Several factors explain this downturn: namely the institutionalization of the White Man's Primary in the farm counties of South Texas, rudeness by whites towards Tejano voters at the polls, demographic shifts such as those which occurred in South Texas, San Antonio, and El Paso that had diluted the former predominance of Tejanos, and the Progressive reaction to nonwhite peoples who supposedly had corrupted democratic rule. To insure honesty in government, the Progressives instituted the poll tax and city-wide elections. The latter practice had as its intent the destruction of bossism, but in the process it eliminated the old ward system under which minorities had commanded at least some sort of representation.[36]

By the 1920s, then, the opportunities that had previously allowed Tejano politicians some chances to hold office were diminished. Machine politics such as those which had emerged in San Antonio in the late nineteenth century now rejected (instead of encouraging) Mexican-American political activity. Tejano voters living in the Alamo City in the 1920s now voted according to the dictates of Anglo bosses if they wished to keep working for the city or county.[37] In the greater South Texas border region, a reversal of bossism took effect. The Progressive offensive weakened the old politicos, and Mexican-American fortunes tumbled commensurately. From the 1880s to 1920, for example, the political boss Jim Wells dispensed patronage to members of propertied Mexican families who occupied several significant elective positions in the city and county. With Wells's downfall in 1920, farmers comprising the new Anglo order sought to minimize Tejano occupation of new political seats. In far off El Paso, Mexican-American politics entered a transitional period during the late 1910s and into the 1920s. Now Texas-Mexican leaders were reduced to intermediaries between the Mexican-American immigrant community and local Anglo government in the city.[38]

About the only Tejano politicians able to weather the changes in the 1910s and 1920s were some in the aforementioned ranch counties of South Texas. The agricultural development which spread throughout the section did not penetrate the westernmost valley counties, and Manuel Guerra, for one, was particularly successful at surviving numerous challenges to his machine (Guerra's sons continued to hold power in Starr County until after World War II). In Duval County, Archie Parr dispensed offices to faithful Tejano supporters (the Parr machine inherited by Archie's son remained entrenched until 1975).[39] Anglo-dominated bossism in lesser degrees extended to other South Texas communities.

Aside from Guerra, the most prominent Tejano politician of South Texas was J. T. Canales. As already noted, this Brownsville attorney had served in the Texas legislature from 1905 to 1910. Reelected to the state legislature in 1916, Canales took stands in support of prohibition and women's suffrage and against the Progressive effort to place restrictions on Texas-Mexican voters. In his boldest crusade, Canales called upon the legislature to investigate the Ranger atrocities against Tejanos and to reorganize the legendary law-enforcement body. Canales failed to persuade the legislature to heed his reforms, although it did reduce the size of the Ranger force. In 1920, Canales retired from the legislature. Not until 1942 were other Tejanos able to win election to the state house.[40]

A New Generation

While political incumbency for Texas Mexicans declined, a young generation of leaders undertook fresh approaches for change, their enthusiasm charged by their United States citizenship and involvement in World War I (either as combat soldiers or civilians).[41] World War I had seemed to offer a serendipitous opportunity for the social improvement of Texas Mexicans. After all, Mexicans had cooperated fully and responded patriotically to the general mobilization. America's concerted effort to integrate all segments of society into support for the war suggested more openness in the future. In the perception of those with an eye towards politics, the future augured long-deferred prospects for social advancement.

Significantly, elements representative of a Tejano middle class, of petty bourgeoisie, veterans, and professionals picked up the struggle when race relations reverted to the pre–World War I standard. In the late 1920s Douglas O. Weeks, a University of Texas political scientist, described this cohort as descending from the old Tejano middle class which went back to the nineteenth century but also from parents with lower-class roots. Some had agrarian backgrounds—that is, they were the offspring of Mexican-American landowners and field hands—who had taken up city residence and benefitted from the educational system in the urban sites. Though most still lived in barrios and entertained a deep appreciation for their Mexican upbringing, they were slightly better off than the majority of other Tejanos and by the 1920s were gaining greater esteem for their states as U.S. citizens.[42]

While the earlier generation of Tejanos had established societies and associations to protect members of the community from injustices, in the 1920s a new generation of activists founded organizations designed to afford Tejanos a greater integration into national life. Such was the intent of the *Orden Hijos de America* (Order Sons of America, or the OSA), founded in San Antonio in October 1921. Compared to precursor groups, the OSA consisted of members born in the United States, extolled loyalty to America, and sought citizen rights through institutional channels. Soon, Sons of America chapters appeared in South Texas from Corpus Christi to Brownsville to Pearsall, fighting for educational equality, the desegregation of public places, the right to serve on juries, and the right to bring suit against a white person (in the 1920s courts refused to hear cases involving Mexican Americans attempting to sue whites).[43]

The OSA splintered soon after its birth, however. Defectors founded the Order Sons of Texas in San Antonio in 1922, and other discontented OSA officers established, in 1927, still another San Antonio group, *Orden Caballeros de America* (the Order Knights of America). These new groups still abided by the philosophy of the OSA and appealed to Tejano citizens to pay their poll tax and vote and encouraged them to become involved in civic and political affairs, stressing the need to be bilingual. This too was the philosophy of another civic organization, the League of Latin American Citizens, founded in the Rio Grande Valley by war veterans J. Luz Saenz and Alonso S. Perales.[44]

Then, concerned Tejano leaders, some of whom had been brought into the war mobilization drive, initiated a unification drive to create a league that would be more effective in the challenge for equality. In 1929, at Corpus Christi, the agents of compromise brought together the various splintered societies—the OSA, Knights of America, and the League of Latin American Citizens—and transformed them into what came to be the League of United Latin American Citizens (LULAC). Several of these World-War-I veterans and civic activists went on to become LULAC officers during the league's early years or served in capacities that enhanced LULAC'S growth into a statewide organization.[45]

ETHNIC TRANSITION

In the era between 1910 and 1930 (actually, until about World War II), loyalties to Mexico and the United States vied for dominion within the Tejano community. Diverse strains of thought manifested those loyalties, and some of these sentiments may be found in the content of community newspapers of the epoch. Representing the Mexican view was *La Prensa*.

More disposed to express the syncretization found in many communities were San Antonio's *El Imparcial de Texas* and Edinburg's *El Defensor*. Edited by Francisco A. Chapa, a Mexico-born Tejano who had achieved both business and political success in Texas, *El Imparcial* voiced the acculturation of many Tejanos and revealed a nascent biculturalism. *El Defensor*, founded in 1930 by Texas-born and college-educated Santiago G. Guzmán, embodied the loyalties of the up-and-coming Tejano middle class that gave its allegiance to the United States. Thus, *El Defensor* emphasized the dual heritage of some Tejanos and reflected a state of mind shaped by growing up in two cultural spheres.[46]

As people do universally, this cohort assimilated the values of the nourishing culture(s): they worked hard, displayed courtesy, respect, and hospitality, cared for their loved ones, sympathized with the downtrodden, and worshiped a Christian being. They also spoke Spanish, esteemed their parents' homeland, identified with or joined mutualistas, ate Mexican dishes, sang corridos, and dressed in a Mexican style, but these same people also spoke English, admired their country of residence, became members of the upstart OSA or LULAC, partook of American foods, listened to mainstream radio hits of the 1920s, and kept abreast of U.S. fashions. Over time, increased numbers of Tejanos would be absorbed into the process of cultural change from a Mexican to an American identity.

CHAPTER SEVEN

To the U.S. Born
1930–1945

The Great Depression

THE Great Depression of the 1930s thrust itself upon Tejanos with vicious force, causing reversals in people's lives or, at best, stifling their chances to improve their condition. Deportation drives and repatriation during the era both tempered the Tejanos' demographic expansion. Deportation involved efforts on the part of the Bureau of Immigration (Department of Labor) and local public and private welfare agencies to expel foreigners who were on relief roles, taking jobs from American citizens, or who resided in the United States illegally. Ordinarily, the deportees would be gathered at some center, then transported to the border by train, truck, or car caravan. Repatriates, on the other hand, departed the state voluntarily for two primary reasons: some found it difficult to eke out a living in a white society that gave fellow Anglos priority in employment and in the allotment of relief funds; or in some cases, the Mexican government offered these people jobs in public works projects (building roads or irrigation facilities) and opened up opportunities for the repatriates to buy land in the motherland. Some 250,000 Mexican immigrants and their children, many of whom had been born in the United States, are estimated to have returned to Mexico from Texas between 1929 and 1939.[1] The 1940 U. S. census placed the figure for Mexican-descent people in Texas at 484,306. But this is a serious undercount, one lower than Roberto M. Villarreal's adjusted figure for 1930.[2]

The crisis of the depression struck Tejano communities in other adverse ways. Wage earners lost their jobs and found it difficult to obtain new employment. At a more personal level, the deportation and repatriation movements caused the separation of families, for many Mexico-born parents were susceptible to extradition. Some had lived in Texas for years and had children who had been born and schooled in the state.

Aside from such problems related directly to the depression, Tejanos still had to endure old forms of bigotry. As in the 1920s, the Anglo notion that Mexicans were somehow dirty and inferior persisted, fostering continued segregation. Thus, many businesses barred Mexicans, fearing that Anglo customers might resent their presence. Catholic churches scheduled separate masses to avoid contact between the two groups. Real-estate agencies followed rules that encouraged ethnic-based separation, and sprouting subdivisions enforced similarly restrictive policies.[3] School boards designated specific accommodations for Mexican children. In the areas of civil rights, society still deterred Texas Mexicans from serving on juries and generally discouraged them from voting.

ECONOMIC AND SOCIAL STANDING

Obviously, the depression impeded economic mobility for the Tejano population. In the rural communities, Tejanos faced lean times as they pursued subsistence by taking onerous and low-paying jobs, often working as maids, cotton pickers, kitchen helpers, slaughter house workers, cannerypersons, and warehousemen. According to surveys conducted in the 1930s and during World War II, poor folks living in South Texas and the Winter Garden areas inhabited small frame dwellings, ordinarily two-room hovels with earthen floors, no windows, and open-pit privies. People cooked in the open since many of the domiciles lacked kitchens. Poverty-related diseases such as diphtheria and tuberculosis thrived under such lamentable living conditions. Midwives ordinarily delivered babies, many of whom died by the age of one as a result of premature birth, pneumonia, influenza, and diarrhea enteritis.[4]

To find steadier or better-paying work, rural Mexicans followed the cotton crop. Even those bound to sharecropping now resorted to migrant work, for as landowners switched to commercial farming, they had no need for full-time, year-round help; they wanted to hire workers only at harvest time.[5]

It was therefore, in the depression years that the so-called "Big Swing" intensified, as workers followed the cotton season from South Texas, through the central portion of the state, then to the West Texas-Panhandle region, then back to their points of origin. Many pickers traveled by car, but scores relied on contractors who negotiated with growers and then trucked the workers to the preagreed destination. In the fields, the *jefe* or *troquero* (as the trucker was called), weighed the cotton sacks, kept track of the number of pounds picked by each field hand, then compensated the migrants from wages paid him by the farmer.[6] In actuality, the migrants' earnings barely offset their travel costs: the Texas State Employment Service in 1938 calculated (on the basis of the prevailing wage of 50 cents per hundred pounds picked) that migrants only made about $37.50 per person during a six-month harvest period.[7]

By routinely making this circuit to the northwestern cotton lands, migrant workers either replenished or founded West Texas and Panhandle Tejano communities. Though treated as a necessary evil in the cotton fields, given little in the way of shelter or toilet facilities, and prohibited from public places in the neighboring communities, many became attached to the places they visited (some of them found employment opportunities in the oil fields of West Texas, performing hard, menial tasks such as digging ditches and cleaning storage tanks). Others, however, remained in the new communities after the termination of the picking season with their entire family, which often included grandparents and grandchildren, simply because they were unable to afford the journey back home.[8]

During the depression living conditions for Tejanos in large urban centers were as wretched as they were in the rural sections. Shacks in the Mexican district of San Antonio lacked proper floors, plumbing, indoor toilet facilities, and electricity. Tuberculosis and intestinal diseases lurked throughout the Mexican quarter menacing every inhabitant. By the time of World War II, the Alamo City had the highest rate of death from tuberculosis in the entire country, almost half of the victims being Mexican Americans. In Houston and Dallas, inquiries made during the war years by the Works Progress Administration (WPA) and newspaper reporters respectively, found Tejanos living in deplorable conditions, some of them managing to support entire families on yearly incomes of about six hundred dollars and residing in cheap, congested, tumble-down houses.[9]

Even as these conditions plagued so many Tejanos, a middle class still endured in cities such as Corpus Christi, Houston, San Antonio, El Paso, and others in the greater South Texas region. According to some estimates, this small middle class of managers, proprietors, salespersons, clerical workers, professionals, and craftsmen comprised about 15 percent of laborers listed in the 1930 census. Exiles and refugees from Mexico, enterprising Mexican-American merchants, and old-line families in the ranch counties of South Texas who still managed to hold on to their lands were among those who composed this "petit bourgeoisie."[10]

LA PATRIA

Several forces between 1930 and 1945 continued to reinforce the ties that Mexican Americans wished to retain with Mexico. Segregation in Texas and the rest of the nation prolonged a Mexican ethnicity. Immigration energized cultural antecedents. "*La patria*," (the motherland, Mexico) moreover, minded the welfare of barrio residents in a foreign land. Efforts by the Mexican government to relocate them in Mexico during the depression, for one thing, touched the sentiments of the lower class as much as it did the small cohorts of ricos and professionals who had taken refuge in Texas during the Mexican Revolution (1910–1920) and still remained interested in the politics of Mexico (many members of this latter group ended up returning to their mother country when Mexico granted a general amnesty during the latter years of the Great Depression). The continued activities of Mexican consuls in Texas also perpetuated ties between Mexico and the unnaturalized, as indeed, these officials who represented Mexico's commercial interests in the state acted vigorously as spokespersons for Mexican nationals, especially in cases in which violent crimes had been inflicted upon them.[11]

Then there were several influences that fanned Mexican nationalist feelings. Available for reading throughout the state were newspapers from Mexico as well as Texas, among the latter being the aforementioned *La Prensa* which reported on news of local and international importance in an attempt to perpetuate linkages between Tejanos and the motherland.[12] Religious occasions, among them nuptials, burials, and church carnivals acted as collective cultural activities for those of different classes. So did the Mexican national holidays of the *Cinco de Mayo*

Top: "Coronado on the High Plains" by Frederic Remington. Copied from a reproduction in *Collier's Magazine*, Dec. 9, 1905. *Institute of Texan Cultures at San Antonio*
Bottom: The *pobladores* (settlers) turned to the environment for materials with which to build homes on the Texas frontier. *Photograph by E. K. Sturdevant, Library of the Daughters of the Republic of Texas at the Alamo, San Antonio, Texas, Institute of Texan Cultures*

Above: Mission Concepcion de Acuna (First Mission) Built 1731. *Prints and Photographs Collection, Barker Texas History Center, University of Texas at Austin*   Below: The *Corrida de la Sandia* (Watermelon Race), part of the celebration of the *Dia de San Juan*. Painting by Theodore Gentilz. *Library of the Daughters of the Republic of Texas at the Alamo, San Antonio, Texas*

Top: *Leñeros*, Tejano wood haulers. *Texas State Library, Austin*
Bottom: The marketplace was the life center of frontier towns. *The San Antonio Museum Association*

Skinning a beef on the Johanna C. Wilhelm Ranch. Stefan de los Santos (with hat on, right) was sheep boss for the ranch. *The Institute of Texan Cultures, San Antonio, Texas*

Tejano and Anglo (French) students and their teacher outside their school in El Carmen, Texas, ca. 1896. *The Institute of Texan Cultures, San Antonio, Texas*

Members of the Theodoro Zambrano family and others in attendance at baby's funeral in early 1900s. Cemetery located in either Karnes or Bee County, Texas. *The Institute of Texan Cultures, San Antonio, Texas*

Colegio Altamirano, 1898. E. E. Mireles & Jovita Gonzalez Mireles Papers, Special Collections & Archives Department, Corpus Christi State University

Above: Interior of *La Prensa* newspaper, ca. 1923–1928.
Right: Unidentified woman holding a parasol with a United States flag used as a backdrop. Attributed to a studio photographer in Beeville, Texas, ca. 1910s.
The Institute of Texan Cultures, San Antonio, Texas

Above: *"Baile de los Gallos"* (the Cock Fight Dance), performed by Alex Moore and his group, at Fiesta La Villita. San Antonio, Texas, 1940s. *The Institute of Texan Cultures, San Antonio, Texas*

Left: Salome Rodríguez, 110 years old, as he joins a caravan of Mexican repatriates on their way back to Mexico from Texas. Published October 19, 1931. *San Antonio Light Collection, The Institute of Texan Cultures, San Antonio, Texas*

Top: Two members of *Conjunto Alamo*: Leandro Guerro (left) and Frank Corrales. Taken at KCOR radio station (in Calcasieu Building) where they played each morning, 6:00 to 6:30, San Antonio, Texas, 1949.
Bottom: Two Boys sitting on a concrete slab outside toilet facilities at West Side (San Antonio) housing complex, 1960s. *The Institute of Texan Cultures, San Antonio, Texas*

Top: Mexican laborers picking cotton and loading it by hand. Near San Benito, Texas, August 1972.

Bottom: Cinco de Mayo celebration at the birthplace of General Ignacio Zaragoza near the La Bahia Presidio, Goliad, Texas, 1972. *The Institute of Texan Cultures, San Antonio, Texas*

José Antonio Navarro, 1795–1871. *Prints and Photographs Collection, Barker Texas History Center, University of Texas at Austin*

Gen. Juan Nepomuceno Cortina. Photo taken by DePlanque, Brownsville, and Matamoros, 1866. *The Institute of Texan Cultures, San Antonio, Texas*

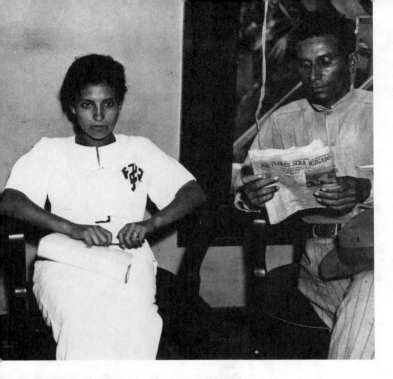

Above: Emma Tenayuca at age 19, in the courthouse waiting to see Mayor Quin about better facilities to distribute relief supplies, San Antonio, Texas, July 16, 1936. *San Antonio Light Collection, Institute of Texan Cultures, San Antonio, Texas*
Left: Dr. Hector García, founder of the American G.I. Forum, ca. 1950. *Dr. Hector García Papers, Special Collections & Archives Department, Corpus Christi State University*

Dr. Americo Paredes *University News and Information Center, University of Texas at Austin*

Representative Henry B. González, 20th District, Texas. *Courtesy Representative González*

and *Diez y Seis de Septiembre*, during which representatives from Mexico, if not the consuls, used the opportunity to remind assembled spectators of their Mexican heritage. Professional and amateur artists organized small-scale companies that presented secular dramas and vaudeville in the various settlements. Also, moving-picture houses showed the screen and stage idols of Mexico, and Spanish-language radio programs broadcast news, commentary, and Mexican songs.[13]

Social and recreative clubs as well as self-help organizations further catered to those who venerated la patria. The 1930s, however, witnessed the decline of many of the mutual aid societies. Repatriation and the increased financial assistance given by the societies to those suffering from the economic hard times reduced the membership. At the same time new federal assistance programs such as Social Security offered similar financial benefits, radio and movies slowly replaced the entertainment functions of the mutualistas' regular meetings, and political clubs after the 1930s siphoned off the more politicized of mutualista members.[14]

To the U.S. Born

The 1930 census in Texas reported about 60 percent of the Mexican-stock people to be United States born (meantime, the immigrant population had declined due to repatriation and deportation efforts). New and powerful forces now confronted young Tejanos who knew only the United States as their country of origin. During the 1920s, for instance, Mexican junior and senior high schools—although segregated—appeared in increasing numbers in order to accommodate more Tejanitos. Students embraced the United States' language, traditions, and fashions, while assimilating other American attitudes about family, faith, and loyalty.[15]

Newspaper stories displayed a similar consciousness. The aforementioned bilingual *El Defensor*, for instance, emphasized that readers take pride both in their Mexican heritage and American citizenship. The newspaper published advertisements for American products and historical bits from the Mexican and American past and encouraged adolescents to consider a university education. Mexican-oriented papers such as *El Continental* of El Paso reported the public spirit displayed by Tejanos on occasions such as the Fourth of July.[16]

U.S.-born-and-raised leaders that included military veterans and a small middle class of entrepreneurs and professionals, at the same time spearheaded notions about adopting American customs and habits into a bicultural heritage, accepting loyalty to the U.S., and gaining access to mainstream institutions on the basis of equality. Articulating such an outlook were what historians call the "Mexican American Generation," some of whom had founded LULAC in 1929. Leaders included Ben Garza, who served as the League's inaugural president (1929–1930), Alonso Perales, LULAC's next national director (1930–1931), and M. C. Gonzales, the organization's third president (1931–1932).[17] From their base in San Antonio, the latter two emerged as the league's organizer-intellectuals of the 1930s. Perales and Gonzales, both attorneys, commanded large followings within Hispanic communities and imparted the LULAC doctrine most persuasively. According to the historian Richard A. García, "Everyone knew them, respected them, and listened to them."[18]

LULAC's commitment was to improving the human condition within the Mexican community regardless of class and even nativity, for though the organization restricted membership to the native born, it did accept those who were naturalized (the organization argued that the foreign born had their defenders in the Mexican consul, but LULAC leaders worked closely with the consuls in cases involving Mexican nationals). Ideologically, LULAC sought to act upon old problems. LULACers still combated the entrenched racist sentiments holding that Mexicans were "unclean," and the Anglo contention that Mexican Americans were not white folks.[19] In response, the organization launched efforts to secure civil liberties and access to opportunity by trying to overturn segregation, for to them the practice stood out as the most personal reminder that Anglo Americans considered Mexican Americans to be second-class citizens.[20] Further, they fought to assert their contention that they were Caucasian, as LULACers did in 1936 when the U.S. Bureau of the Census ruled that Mexicans be identified as "non-whites." Protest from LULAC councils across the state forced the Census Bureau to retract the categorization. Similar pressure exerted upon the Social Security Administration that same year forced the Social Security Board to accept the application of Mexican Americans as white.[21]

Similarly, the League worked doggedly to pry open more opportunities in education. It initially challenged school segregation in the case of

Independent School District, et al v. *Salvatierra* (1931) arguing for an end to the deliberate segregation of Mexican children in Del Rio. A Texas Court of Civil Appeals ruled that arbitrary segregation was unjust, but sided with school officials who contended that the students' retention of the Spanish language made segregation necessary.[22] Without funds to follow up on *Salvatierra*, LULAC pursued other tactics, such as going before school districts and conferring with administrators to argue for better teaching for Mexican-American children. To disseminate their faith in education, LULACers organized evening schools in barrios and conducted meetings that focused on the topic of U.S. citizenship. They also undertook fundraisers to subsidize the education of good student prospects who might become skilled workers, lawyers, doctors, and teachers.[23]

POLITICS IN THE 1930S

Little political remonstrance in the vein of the Primer Congreso Mexicanista or the Plan de San Diego occurred between 1930 and 1945, although Tejanos did launch reform drives to induce change. Such was the case in San Antonio where in 1934 a diverse assemblage of community-oriented societies, behind the leadership of Eleuterio Escobar, united under the name of *La Liga Pro-Defensa Escolar* (School Improvement League) to reject segregation and persuade school officials to bring better facilities and improved education to the Mexican settlement in the city's West Side. Although it won concessions from the San Antonio School Board in 1935 to build three new elementary schools and improve existing structures, the impact of the depression and the dawning of World War II stifled further action, and the League entered a temporary hiatus.[24]

   Also appearing during this time was the *Confederación de Organizaciones Mexicanas y Latino Americanas* (Confederation of Mexican and Latin American Organizations, COMLA) founded in the late 1930s in the Gulf Coast area (there apparently existed a parallel organization with a similar name in El Paso). The Houston/Galveston COMLA intended to act as an umbrella organization for the various lodges, societies, and civic groups throughout Texas, and though the prime movers were the Mexican consuls in these two East Texas cities, it purported to be a confederation that would work towards the well being of all Mexicans as well as "Latin Americans" (as it called Mexican Americans). In its early years, the COMLA initiated serious efforts to overturn racist policies, such as discrimination and Jim Crow segregation. It never succeeded, however, in accomplishing its goal of uniting the Gulf Coast's several societies and civic groups in a common struggle.[25]

In the realm of electoral politics, things remained near the depth reached during the preceding two decades. This rule applied particularly to the regional and state levels, though campaigners could be found seeking these offices. In 1942, the first Tejanos since J. T. Canales won election to the state legislature: Augustín Celaya from Brownsville and John C. Hoyo from Béxar County.[26]

Political movements by Tejanos in this era were not absent however. They turned up, in fact, wherever reformers founded LULAC chapters, notes Richard A. García: in San Antonio, a city that contained an activist Tejano middle class and a large Mexican population; in South Texas towns like Brownsville, Corpus Christi, Kingsville, Alice, and Laredo, and in West Texas sites such as San Angelo, though this last region of the state lacked the leadership found in South Texas, perhaps because of its relative isolation from the rest of Texas or perhaps because of the numerical disadvantage of Tejanos there. The famous *Escuadrón Volante*, or "Flying Squadron" composed of the League's San Antonio leaders, made frequent trips throughout the state in order to help establish new councils and spread the LULAC word. By the beginning of World War II, LULAC had reached its pinnacle of strength, but when LULACers enlisted in the United States military service in 1941, LULAC's ranks were reduced.[27]

In the decade of the 1930s, also, LULAC members took it upon themselves to perform a variety of civic and political responsibilities. They participated in Red Cross and Community Chest fundraisers, volunteered as leaders for the Boy Scouts and Girl Scouts and the Salvation Army, sponsored programs such as Latin American Health Week, and organized PTA's in barrio public schools. Committed to increasing U.S. citizenship and voting registration among Tejanos and to securing adequate representation in public office, LULACers went before city commissioners to press for the resolution of specific problems, organized assemblies, acted as intermediaries between the Mexican enclaves and bureaucrats, and conducted poll-tax raising drives.[28] Though claiming LULAC to be a nonpolitical entity, individual members nonetheless joined political groups that went by names such as the League of Loyal Americans (in San Antonio) or the Latin Sons of Texas (Houston).

Through these political organizations, Tejanos protested their impoverished conditions in the Mexican quarters, confronted local businesses that did not hire Mexicans, introduced political candidates (both Anglo and Mexican) to Texas-Mexican voters, endorsed slates of office seekers, and joined in presidential campaigns such as that of Franklin D. Roosevelt. LULACers abided by a prescribed code of conduct and avoided extreme methods of protest, militant confrontation, strikes, and marches.[29]

Women joined in the various LULAC programs, for in 1932, LULAC incorporated women's auxiliaries. Mexican-American women members in that era resisted the LULAC male notion that wives belonged at home, and though they did not share equality with male LULACers, women made important contributions to their communities (albeit in deeds closely related to "women's work"). They assisted in orphanages and health clinics, sponsored youth activities, participated in registration drives, raised scholarship funds, and taught English and helped Mexican nationals study for U.S. citizenship.

Among the most prominent women to serve LULAC in the era were Mrs. J. C. Machuca of El Paso and Alice Dickerson Montemayor of Laredo. Firm in her thinking that women should share authority with their male counterparts, Machuca organized the League's first Ladies Council, assumed the office of Ladies Organizer General, and indefatigably worked to establish more Ladies Councils,[30] among them one in Laredo which brought into LULAC its first feminist, Mrs. Montemayor. Between 1937 and 1940, Alice Dickerson Montemayor served on several national posts, advocating (through articles published in *LULAC News*) independent insights that questioned notions of male dominance. She also favored a strategy that women should work in unison to improve the general status of other women. In the 1930s, however, male-dominated LULAC councils were not disposed to hear such points of view. For inexplicable reasons, Montemayor left LULAC in 1940.[31]

LABOR PROTEST

The wellsprings for the subdued but undaunted struggle for worker's objectives in the 1930s lay in the hardships of the masses, on renewed efforts by leftists to recruit Mexicans into labor unionism, and, in the agricultural sector, in New Deal labor legislation that neglected farm workers.[32] Though most mainstream labor unions still excluded Mexicans from membership, Tejanos in various parts of the state addressed the need to find remedies to conditions that racked commonfolk Mexican-American and immigrant laborers. In West Texas, where many Tejanos engaged in sheep shearing as a means of livelihood, 750 members of the Sheep Shearers' Union of North America struck against low wages and exploitive employment practices in 1934, though threats, strikebreakers, arrests, and vigilante harassment defeated the movement.[33]

The more vigorous labor-protest activity, expectedly, was to be found in South Texas. In Crystal City, for example, spinach workers joined the Catholic Workers Union in 1930 and reached a settlement with local growers and processors concerning working arrangements, low wages, and child labor. In Laredo, *La Asociación de Jornaleros* (Association of Journeymen Workers), an independent union founded in 1933, led an abortive strike of harvesters in the irrigated farms near the city in 1935. The next year, upon being chartered as the Agricultural Workers' Union No. 20212 by the AFL, the body continued pushing to organize similar locals in other farming sectors of the state.[34]

Then in 1938, the United Cannery, Agricultural, Packing, and Allied Workers of America (UCAPAWA) located operations in the Lower Rio Grande Valley, though efforts to organize agricultural hands did not yield significant victories. Following a period of decline, UCAPAWA resurfaced in the greater South Texas region to recognize Tejano truck drivers, shed packers, and field hands belonging to Spinach Workers' Union Local No. 87. In 1942, the union won a slight pay increase from producers in the Mathis area, but then faltered. The following year, the Texas Fruit and Vegetable Workers' Union Local 35 (also UCAPAWA chartered) attempted to organize the citrus fruit and vegetable industry labor force in the Lower Rio Grande Valley. The local won some concessions but little is known of its existence after 1945.[35]

Similar efforts at union organization were undertaken in the urban areas. In El Paso, workers at the major smelters and refineries joined the International Union of Mine, Mill, and Smelter Workers in 1939 and by 1946 had earned union recognition, maximum hour and wage benefits, and other privileges.[36] In 1938, at the height of the pecan-shelling season, Tejano pecan shellers belonging to the Texas Pecan Shelling Workers' Union (chartered by UCAPAWA) executed a walkout of the

San Antonio plants led by the twenty-two-year-old San Antonio-born union organizer Emma Tenayuca. In solidarity, the protestors demanded improved wages and working conditions and an end to child labor. But police used force, mass arrests, and harassment of the unionists to destroy the movement. Some gains were made, but companies instituted machine operations shortly after, thus offsetting the concessions. In the Gulf Coast city of Houston, also, Mexicans joined initiatives by UCAPAWA to organize cotton compresses in 1941. In a contract negotiated with management, workers won overtime pay, time off on ethnic holidays (such as Diez y Seis de Septiembre) and a salary increase.[37]

Women played significant roles in the unionist fervor of the era (according to one historian, women participants in San Antonio outnumbered men in activities that challenged subsistence wages and abject conditions in the workplace).[38] In 1933 and 1934, Tejana cigar rollers and tobacco strippers in San Antonio left their jobs at the Finck Cigar Company, complaining of ill-furnished bathrooms, poor plumbing, and an unhealthy environment. Scabs broke the strike, so management never met workers' grievances. In San Antonio, also, Tejanas, joined the International Ladies Garment Workers Union (ILGWU)—in 1939, 80 percent of the 1,400 San Antonio women who belonged to this union were Mexicans—and while their strikes against local plants often ended unsuccessfully, a strike in 1937 against the Shirlee Frocks Company (manufacturer of infants' attire) did produce union recognition and the concession of a 20-cents-an-hour wage. ILGWU organizing of Tejanas in San Antonio continued until the war years, and many of the garment workers came under the protection of union contracts, at least until the 1940s when union activity across the state became exhausted. In Laredo, Tejana home workers organized *La Unión de Costureras* (the Seamstresses Union) in 1934, then sought affiliation with the ILGWU in 1936 to win decent wages and improved working conditions.[39]

In the end, the pre–World War II union movement among Texas Mexicans made little headway. Too many factors acted to prevent victories, among them labor surpluses, the precarious nature of the economy, the antiunion climate pervasive throughout Texas, and the basic contention among Anglos that Mexicans did not deserve better working conditions. Such factors would continue to inhibit union organizing after World War II.[40]

WORLD WAR II

World War II hardly opened up new opportunities for Texas Mexicans. The call for cooperation touched numerous barrios and ranchos and mobilization brought Texas Mexicans close to Anglos in a common cause of security and survival, but economic advancement for Tejanos still proved elusive. Very few Mexican Americans found work in war-related industries, and those who were hired performed common or un-skilled labor. The paltry job openings that did open up to the Mexican-American community had more to do with the military emergency than with the relaxation of Jim Crow attitudes. The exigencies of the war produced the Fair Employment Practices Committee (FEPC) to moni-tor job discrimination among federal agencies and private businesses contracting with the government, though not until 1943 did the FEPC undertake operations. Companies then began promoting Mexican Americans into the semiskilled and skilled openings, but even that was done grudgingly.[41]

As for a contribution to the war, Texas Mexicans joined up with pa-triotic zeal. Tejanos born and raised in the larger cities as well as in rural hamlets and small towns of the state answered the called to arms for a variety of reasons: military duty expedited naturalization for the foreign-born, scant numbers met the criteria for draft deferments, some looked at the armed forces as a way out of poverty, and most genuinely believed in the ideals of their country.[42] At the battle front, they saw duty in integrated companies, though others belonged to all-Mexican-American units like the Company E. 141st Regiment of the 36th (Texas) Division, which fought with distinction in the European the-ater. Five Texas Mexicans—José M. López, Macario García, Cleto L. Rodríguez, Luciano Adams, and Silvestre Herrera—won the Congres-sional Medal of Honor for heroism in Europe and the Far East. While in the service, Tejanos came to know a treatment by whites that was more tolerant than that prevalent in their hometowns.[43]

KEEPING THE FAITH

If the 1920s turned out to be years that stifled the World-War-I genera-tion's hope for integration, the Great Depression era dampened those hopes even further. Unemployment during the 1930s inflicted greater misfortune upon Texas Mexicans than it did upon the general society, not only because preferences for possible job openings went to white folks, but because society questioned Tejanos' U.S. citizenship—and thus eligibility for jobs. Indeed, to be Mexican made one a candidate for possible deportation. Jim Crow, moreover, feasted on intolerant times. Disfranchisement, enduring patterns of segregation, and sub-standard schooling further aggravated the age's misery. The "Big Swing" across the state may have been an adventure only to the young. For parents migrant work seemed to lead only towards uncertainty.

The pre–World War II years produced imaginative responses from Tejano communities, however. The new depth of desperation moved Tejano leaders of every political stripe to act on behalf of the forlorn. Those concerned with working-class compatriots sought to help them through means as diverse as the imposition of impromptu work stop-pages, affiliation with the AFL and also the Communist party, and even violence. In the bigger cities, alarmed Mexican-American spokesmen organized different types of groups in an effort to counter their people's nagging woes. San Antonio established the Liga Pro-Defensa Escolar. Houston and El Paso addressed the needs of their people through COMLA. These cities, and several smaller communities throughout the state, founded LULAC councils to overturn barriers that circumscribed equality. The political strategy of the 1930s would be carried on by "Latin Americans" in the postwar era.

CHAPTER EIGHT

"Latin Americans" in the Postwar Era 1945–1960

WORLD WAR II exerted profound influences on the state of Texas. In its wake, the war for democracy produced several years of prosperity as returning veterans and civilian defense workers hastened to spend incomes accumulated during the conflict. Industrialization rode a new wave as oil refining, chemical and petrochemical production, and defense industry plants surged in the 1950s. Cities burgeoned, moreover, as people from rural areas and small communities gravitated toward urban centers. As of 1960, 63.4 percent of the Texas's 9.6 million people made the state's metropolitan counties their place of residence.[1]

On the other hand, some features of the Texas landscape did not change much, at least not until the late 1950s. Politics, for one, retained its conservative bent. On the one hand, many Texas Democrats preferred disassociation with the national party's support for unionism and civil rights, while on the other, Texas Republicans refused to relax their opposition to constitutional liberties and welfare assistance. In race relations, the strength of Jim Crow sentiments led to the passage of several segregationist laws in 1956–1957, and while their purpose was to prop up long-standing discrimination against African Americans, by implication they extended to those of Mexican descent.[2] Meantime, right-wing extremism prevailed as Wisconsin Senator Joseph McCarthy's campaign against Communists at the national level found supporters throughout Texas. Reactionaries demanded the removal of controversial books from libraries, the dismissal of teachers considered too liberal for local standards, and the suppression of left-wing ideas.[3]

Nonetheless, Texas began to take new directions in the postwar era (especially towards the late 1950s) that opened up fresh possibilities for Texas Mexicans. In that period, the old agrarian order long committed to the subordination of Tejanos lost the political advantage to urban commercial interests, farm ownerships made a transformation from individually owned concerns into mechanized corporate entities, and many who had been field hands moved to the cities where industry offered better wages. By the mid–1950s, furthermore, McCarthyism was on the wane, and no longer a political issue handicapping "foreigners" from pursuing the American dream.[4]

Texas-Mexican Society at Midcentury

The interruption in population growth that occurred during the 1930s ended during World War II and the 1950s; the number of Tejanos now increased from about 1,000,000 in 1950 to 1,400,000 in 1960. According to the census of 1960, 86 percent of white persons of Spanish surname in Texas were native born.[5]

Like the rest of the state's population, the Texas-Mexicans in the post–World War II years became more urbanized. During the war, a rural area–to city migration had occurred due to rising occupational prospects and demand for laborers in the new urban industrial sectors, and improved wages in the 1950s persuaded others to relocate. Farm hands were also pushed out of bucolic work by the transformation then underway: new mechanization and improved techniques permitted farmers to produce more without the previous reliance on manual labor.[6] Whereas 57 percent of Texas Mexicans resided in urban areas in 1940, 78 percent of Texas Mexicans did so by the 1950s, and the pattern accelerated thereafter.[7] By 1960, some 30,000 Mexican Americans lived in Dallas, 75,000 in Houston, and 243,000 in San Antonio (by then, only Los Angeles, California, had more Mexicans than the Alamo City). In the 1950s, Texas Mexicans made up 50 percent of El Paso's population.[8]

In their socioeconomic standing, close to 75 percent of Texas-Mexican males remained members of the proletariat. According to the

1950 U.S. census, Tejanos lived on a yearly median income of about $1,000. Anglo Americans at that time made twice that much.[9]

Many Tejano city dwellers faced the same conditions that had vexed their parents and grandparents. These included neglect from city government concerning squalid living conditions, high infant death-rates, and rampant scourges such as tuberculosis, diarrhea, and typhus. The 1950 U.S. census identified 33 percent of urban homes owned or rented by Tejanos in the state as being substandard.[10]

In the rural areas, living conditions for Tejanos were even more bleak. Seasonal work in the cotton fields for which farmers paid around $1.25 per hundredweight (that is, per hundred pounds picked) remained an option for survival, though families participating in the migrant cycle made less than $400 per year during the 1950s.[11] In face of the lean wage rates and competition from Mexican illegals (called "wetbacks" during the era, or *mojados* in Spanish), whose numbers mounted during World War II because of alleged labor shortages in state agriculture, Tejanos took off for the Midwest in hordes. There, lodging in the sugar beet and tomato fields was as primitive as in Texas, though wage rates exceeded those in the home quarters.[12]

Others joined the intrastate migration, either in family units or with troqueros. They responded to the beckonings of farmers for whom they had previously worked, then followed the well-traveled route from South Texas, through the Coastal Bend area, into Central Texas, and then to West Texas. Along the way, they encountered all too familiar problems: having to improvise to find shelter (usually in the fields but more likely beneath the protection of bridges or deserted sheds or chicken coops), entering towns that lacked parking areas for trucks as well as bathing facilities and toilets, and facing inadequate means to battle disease, especially dysentery, due to the poor sanitary measures afforded them. Those who returned to their hometowns (many did not, augmenting Tejano communities along the migrant trail) awaited the new planting and picking seasons by working in whatever jobs became available. The migrant workers' children meantime, tried to obtain schooling for a few months in the spring.[13]

On the other hand, the resilient Tejano middle class continued to be augmented, primarily in the urban sites. The 1940s and 1950s constituted watershed years for Mexicans in terms of opportunities for socioeconomic advancement. In 1950, middle-class categories (professionals, managers, proprietors, clerical, sales, and craftsmen) for men rose to 25 percent, up from the 15 percent reported for 1930.[14]

Labor Movements in a Conservative Age

Texas-Mexican labor organization declined somewhat in the postwar era. As noted, labor historians consider the era of the 1930s to have been one of acute union activity; that intensity lessened between 1945 and 1960 because of the probusiness sentiments that seemed endemic to the state, apprehension among activists of being branded Communist agitators or labor racketeers and being incarcerated for un-American activities, the many options available to employers to suppress walkouts, and because unions discouraged Tejano workers from membership. In the case of the ILGWU, for instance, the national office showed reluctance to invest money in Texas to organize and train union leaders. The result was more workers in the state's garment factories during the 1950s but a decline in union numbers.[15]

Overall, it appears that the postwar era became one of setbacks in the face of self-organization. In El Paso, the Amalgamated Clothing Workers struck for higher wages that same year, but the company imported Mexican nationals to break the walk-out.[16] In 1948, workers at the Rio Grande Valley Gas Company in Harlingen, Texas, sought to organize a union, but management hired illegal aliens to replace the organizers and their supporters.[17] Then, in 1951, Mexican-American women garment workers belonging to the ILGWU staged a walkout of a Houston plant, but the factory went out of business shortly after.[18] In early 1959, Mexican Americans struck against the Tex-Son Company of San Antonio, which specialized in the making of young men's wear. Beating of strikers ensued, but workers and sympathizers picketed merchants carrying Tex-Son products and appealed to religious groups and fellow unions in San Antonio for assistance. Ultimately replacements and anti-labor legislation weakened the job action, and by 1962 the strike had foundered.[19]

Postwar Politics

Though World War II was very much a watershed in opening up new opportunities for Texas Mexicans, civil rights between 1945 and the late

1950s did not come to Tejanos automatically. With the war's end, white society once again regressed toward old attitudes. One West Texan veteran, for instance, groaned that he and fellow G.I.'s had not fought Hitler to have "ill-smelling Mexicans" now clamor for integration.[20] Public establishments still refused to serve Tejanos, even recently discharged soldiers, among them Medal of Honor winners. White neighborhoods, eating places, picture shows, tonsorial shops, swimming pools, and even hospitals were considered off-limits to Mexican Americans. Throughout the state, police authorities and other law enforcement agencies such as the Border Patrol—an agency of the Immigration and Naturalization Service responsible for keeping immigrants from entering the U.S. illegally—regularly reminded Tejanos of their second-class citizenship through disparagement or intimidation.[21] On the job, a similar retreat from the racial tolerance exhibited during the war years occurred. Employment opportunities for Tejanos diminished quickly. Those who had occupied skilled positions during the war now faced demotion, or even dismissal, while new employees found little available beside unskilled tasks.[22] In South Texas, the press, influential businessmen, and farmers no longer preoccupied themselves with fair-play for Texas Mexicans, and although Governor Coke Stevenson in 1943 created the Good Neighbor Commission to better relations between Texas and both Mexico and Mexican Americans, the agency was staffed by personnel with little commitment to alleviating discrimination.[23]

Politically, Texas Mexicans in the immediate postwar years still had to pay the poll tax and cope with other voting and office-holding restrictions. They were handicapped by the lack of necessary funds to field candidates from their own neighborhoods and had to campaign against Anglos who felt politics to be their exclusive domain. Moreover, bossism still survived at midcentury. In South Texas, businessmen and farmers possessed enough economic power to control the votes.[24] The political condition of Texas Mexicans thus remained at a level only slightly improved since the 1920s, when the Anglo-American domination of the border towns from South Texas to Far West Texas dealt a crushing blow to the Mexican-American presence in public offices.

But a resurgence of Tejanos in politics occurred by the 1950s, as "progressive" Anglo business leaders in the cities stood up to the power of the old guard that dominated the machines. The challengers tried to incorporate middle-class Mexican Americans into local government so as to establish a climate conducive to business expansion. In San Antonio, especially, power brokers by the early 1950s sought to enlist blacks and Mexican Americans for progressive slates, though Tejanos who did win by tacit agreement of these movers and shakers often found it difficult once in office to work effectively for Tejano causes because of their ties to Anglo sponsors.[25] However, in 1956, an independent grass-roots campaign produced the election of Henry B. González to the Texas legislature, making him the first Tejano to serve in the state senate in the twentieth century. Voter registration and a get-out-the-vote campaign in El Paso led to the election in 1957 of Raymond Telles, the city's first Mexican-American mayor. He won reelection two years later without opposition.[26]

Compared to the other sections of the state, South Texas and Far West Texas had produced more prominent civic leaders, been the primary centers of activism in the Tejano community, and generally held an edge on the number of Tejanos in office. Indeed, of the six Tejanos in the state house in 1960, two were from San Antonio, one from El Paso, and the other three from the South Texas border area. At midcentury, therefore, it was still difficult to organize Mexican Americans in the rural counties of West and Northwest Texas due to their physical isolation.[27]

Renewed Struggles for a Better Life

Out of World War II and the Korean War emerged politically minded Mexican-American veterans who set out on a concentrated course to erase the inequalities that their people faced. The military experience had defined for them the meaning of citizenship and exposed them to the inconsistencies of a country that espoused equality but did not practice it. In San Antonio, therefore, civic leaders took activist stances through organizations such as the Loyal American Democrats, the West Side Voters League, and the Alamo Democrats. Eleuterio Escobar revitalized La Liga Pro-Defensa Escolar in 1947 to again press for equal and adequate educational facilities and more educational opportunities for Mexican-American children.[28]

Also organized in San Antonio that year by business and professional men was the Pan American Progressive Association (PAPA). As a nonpartisan entity, it sought ways in which to improve the lives of the Mexican-descent population of the city, including the integration of residential areas in San Antonio. But PAPA's life appears not to have extended beyond the early 1950s.[29]

In Corpus Christi, World War II veteran Dr. Hector P. García in 1948 founded what evolved into the most vigorous advocacy organization of the postwar, the American G.I. Forum. Originally established in an effort to expedite federal benefits for Mexican-American ex-servicemen, the G.I. Forum attained a new standing in 1949 with the famous Félix Longoria affair at Three Rivers, Texas. When the local funeral home refused to hold services for Longoria, a slain World War II soldier, Dr. García publicized the incident—which gained nationwide attention—as one more example of entrenched racial intolerance in the rural regions of South Texas. Through the intervention of Senator Lyndon B. Johnson of Texas, Longoria's remains were interred at Arlington National Cemetery.

The courageous stand that the G.I. Forum took on the incident vaulted the group into the role of spokesperson for disadvantaged Mexican Americans.[30] G.I. Forum chapters from across the state now united with LULAC councils to press for sociopolitical advances. Involved in these struggles were leaders from the 1930s and World War II years, among them Alonso Perales, M. C. Gonzales, J. T. Canales, James Tafolla, George I. Sánchez, and Carlos E. Castañeda. But joining them in the era between 1945 and 1960 (and after for that matter), were Gus García, Ed Idar, Cristobal Alderete, John J. Herrera, and of course, Dr. García.

Also part of this activist cadre were women from the two organizations. Representatives of Ladies G.I. Forum Auxiliaries and Ladies LULAC Councils engaged in programs established to: buy milk tickets for children whose parents suffered from tuberculosis; purchase glasses for needy students; distribute toys to the poor at Christmas time; raise funds to provide clothing for children in hospitals; and donate money to the March of Dimes and the Polio Drive. Alongside men, women helped back Little League baseball clubs to aid adolescents in acquiring a positive attitude for themselves; they worked in poll-tax-raising drives and rallies and were often the prime figures in the establishment of new councils throughout the country by spearheading efforts to integrate public accommodations and voice the concerns of Mexican-American women. Many gained recognition within their respective organizations as exemplary models of commitment to the cause of Mexican-American rights.[31]

SCHOOL DESEGREGATION EFFORTS

For years, activists had noted the lack of education for Tejanos as the major stumbling block towards the people's progress. The presence of inferior "Mexican schools," especially, stigmatized children as being less than full-fledged citizens, hindered their ability to learn the English language, and impeded their participation in matters relevant to the community.[32] Because middle-class leaders understood schooling to be a gateway to social betterment, they sponsored efforts to educate Tejano children by means that included back-to-school drives, public service announcements over radio, community rallies, teenage hops, and king and queen balls.[33]

The middle-class leaders also undertook legal measures, according to historian Guadalupe San Miguel's study of the Texas-Mexican campaign for educational equality. Following World War II (before the founding of the G.I. Forum), LULAC took the lead in seeking legal reversals to educational wrongs. In California, the League contested the pattern of segregation in *Méndez* v. *Westminster School District* (1945), and the subsequent ruling by the Ninth Federal District Court in Los Angeles—that segregation of Mexican-American children indeed infringed on guarantees made by the Fourteenth Amendment—had inspired the drive to desegregate schools in the Lone Star State.[34] Therefore, in January 1948, Minerva Delgado and several parents in Central Texas, counseled by LULAC, alleged that school segregation in the region was in breach of the Constitution. Soon after, the G.I. Forum closed ranks behind LULAC with moral support and financial contributions garnered from across the state. In *Delgado* v. *Bastrop ISD* (1948), a district court agreed with the aggrieved plaintiffs, declaring that separating students in different buildings violated the law.[35]

Despite this legal pronouncement and supportive regulations issued by the state superintendent of public instruction to integrate, most school districts generally overlooked the *Delgado* decision. Undaunted, Mexican-American leaders took other segregation cases to court, including the significant *Hernández* v. *Driscoll Consolidated Independent School District* (1957). In their complaint, LULAC and the G.I. Forum argued that the segregation of Mexican-American children in the first two grades and their subsequent detention at that level for a total of four years was an unreasonable practice predicated on notions about race or ancestry. In January 1957, a federal district court agreed with the charge. Despite such significant victories, school districts devised ways of evading court orders. These included gerrymandering districts (dividing districts unfairly to insure segregation), building schools for specific neighborhoods, and offering freedom-of-choice plans that allowed Anglos to select the school they preferred to have their children attend.[36]

The commitment to educational matters produced, in 1957, what came to be known as the "Little Schools of the 400." The brainchild of National LULAC President Félix Tijerina, the program, first implemented in Ganado, Texas, by seventeen-year-old Isabel Verver, sought to have preschool Tejanos learn four hundred English key words and phrases that would allow them to succeed in their first year in school. Implemented initially in Jackson County, the project proved so popular by 1958 that the Houston entrepreneur enacted similar programs in other parts of the state and gained the endorsement of Price Daniel, the governor of Texas. The next year, the state legislature funded Tijerina-type schools to the tune of $1,300,000. The concept of the "Little Schools of the 400" survived into the 1960s, though budget cutting undermined it by the middle of that decade. The federal government, however, later modeled its Head Start program on Tijerina's creation.[37]

HERNÁNDEZ V. TEXAS

LULAC and the G.I. Forum also joined forces to have Mexican Americans recognized as a *class* whose rights Texans transgressed. To this end, Gus García took the case (with the assistance of attorneys John J. Herrera and James de Anda) of Pete Hernández, who had been accused of murdering Joe Espinosa in Edna, Texas, in 1950. In his motion against the state, García contended that the omission of Mexican Americans from jury service in Jackson County violated their right as a *class* to equal protection under the law. Hernández was tried nonetheless, and the jury rendered a guilty verdict and condemned him to life imprisonment.

The United States Supreme Court agreed to hear *Hernández* v. *State of Texas* and LULAC and the G.I. Forum members supplied the needed funds for the attorneys' Washington stay. In May 1954, the high court agreed unanimously that Texas laws that discriminated ostensibly on the basis of *class* (or against "other whites," such as Mexicans) did in fact defy the rights and assurance granted by the Constitution. Hernández was retried and again found guilty (though given a lesser sentence), but the Supreme Court's decision was far-reaching as it acknowledged that Tejanos (to whom Jim Crow laws did not ostensibly apply) had long been the victim of discriminatory treatment. The verdict did not change race relations in Texas immediately, but future generations of Tejanos would profit from its implications.[38]

THE ACSSP

In the background of such efforts to protect the legal rights of Mexican Americans in the United States existed an organization recently redis-covered by the historian Ricardo Romo called the American Council of Spanish-Speaking People (ACSSP). Founded in 1951 by the educator George I. Sánchez, ACSSP pursued litigation in the area of civil rights and assisted sister civic action groups in other parts of the United States. With monies received from the American Civil Liberties Union, it fi-nanced several civil rights cases during its brief period of existence, among them *Hernández* v. *State of Texas* (1954) and *Hernández* v. *Dris-coll Consolidated Independent School District* (1957). By the late 1950s, however, the ACSSP faced decline as Sánchez and other members of the Council found less time to dedicate to the organization and funds be-came more difficult to acquire. In 1959, the ACSSP passed into history, having set an example as a courageous attempt to utilize the legal system as a recourse for redress on behalf of Spanish-speaking Americans.[39]

LOS DEL OTRO LADO

In seeking to improve the lives of Mexican Americans after World War II, both LULAC and the G.I. Forum resisted what Tejanos of the era referred to as the "Wetback Problem." In the eyes of these organiza-tions, the presence of *braceros* (day laborers from Mexico brought to the U.S. on contract) and "wetbacks" cheapened wages for Texas-Mexican residents, supplanted them from agricultural jobs, intensified health problems in the colonias, and generally gave "Latin Americans" (the preferred self-referent used by Mexican-American leaders circa the 1930s to the 1950s to combat the image held by Anglos that Tejanos were not "Americans") a bad name. The braceros were part of an official labor agreement negotiated between the United States and Mexico dur-ing the war years to provide field hands for United States farm estates facing labor shortages. Although Mexico had banned the movement of braceros into Texas because of the state's well-known racism, it relented in 1947 and removed Texas from the "blacklist." Illegal entrants ("wetbacks"), on the other hand, had arrived in Texas after 1942 in response to the state's great demand for farm workers and continued to be preferred by growers as they could be hired without bureaucratic interference and could be easily exploited by avaricious farm managers.[40]

To combat the "Wetback Problem," the G.I. Forum and LULAC lobbied to extradite illegals, to terminate the bracero program, and to have the border better patrolled in order to halt unauthorized crossings into Texas. In 1953, the G.I. Forum published an investigative report titled *What Price Wetbacks?* as part of its ongoing efforts to combat the presence of undocumented workers. The pamphlet illuminated the exploitation of wetback labor and explained the effects these laborers had upon health standards in border communities. The survey further faulted law authorities for a lax enforcement of the immigration statutes.[41]

Politicians seemed indifferent to the Forum's concerns (preferring to ignore the issue because it helped the nation's growers maintain a supply of cheap labor), but the public ultimately became alarmed over the "wetback menace." With popular support, therefore, the Immigration and Naturalization Service in July 1954, ventured upon a widesweeping campaign called "Operation Wetback." In corroboration with local and federal authorities, the Border Patrol mounted raids into the rural areas of Texas to arrest illegals and evict them to Mexico. The drives affected many American citizens of Mexican descent who witnessed close relatives forcibly repatriated. The American G.I. Forum and LULAC both countenanced the project, though they did make attempts to insure that the rights of the Texas-Mexican citizens were respected. But their stand caused friction within the ranks of the Tejano community, leading many to question the sensitivity of the Forumeers, LULACers, and other supporters of the xenophobic campaigns.[42]

Academicians and Writers

Previous generations of Texas Mexicans had contributed to a literary past, some in English, some in Spanish. Juan Seguín and José Antonio Navarro had both left memoirs, and a small number of Tejanos had also penned autobiographies. Lay historians had put together informal histories to note the role Tejanos played in the Texas saga. Other writers had dealt with ongoing concerns of importance to the Tejano community. Spanish-language newspapers regularly printed creative literature, and Tejano authors of fiction had published through other outlets.

In the postwar era, academicians, intellectuals, and others with a talent for composition added to that literary record. Noteworthy writers include historians, the most renowned being Dr. Carlos E. Castañeda. A professor of history at the University of Texas until his death in 1957, Castañeda wrote numerous works during the period between the Great Depression and the 1950s that sought to explain the Spanish/Mexican contribution to Texas history, among them the now classic, seven volume study, *Our Catholic Heritage* (7 vols; Austin: Von Boeckmann-Jones, Co., 1936–1958). His lifetime bibliography of twelve books and seventy-eight articles contributed to Texas and borderlands scholarship by identifying the debt American history owed to Spain and Mexico.[43]

Dr. Américo Paredes, a University of Texas folklore teacher, writer, and poet educated in the Brownsville schools, in 1958 published *"With His Pistol in His Hand": A Border Ballad and Its Hero* (Austin: University of Texas, 1958), a book studying the kinship between the corrido and the real historical events surrounding the episode of Gregorio Cortéz. The lay historian Mercurio Martínez coauthored *The Kingdom of Zapata* (San Antonio: The Naylor Co., 1953), and Cleofas Calleros in numerous pieces preserved the history of Spaniards and Mexicans in the El Paso Valley.[44]

New Mexico-born-and-educated George I. Sánchez, who taught in the Department of History and Philosophy of Education at the University of Texas from 1940 to 1972 (when he passed away), authored or edited some fifty books, monographs, and special reports as well as some eighty articles, many of which dealt with his deep concern with the quality of education for Mexican-American students. As a graduate school professor at the University of Texas, Sánchez directed in excess of sixty-five Master's theses and twenty-eight doctoral dissertations, and he taught as a visiting professor in universities both in the United States and overseas.[45]

In the early 1930s, Jovita González became one of the first Mexican Americans to publish English-language translations of traditional Tejano storytelling, submitting articles to various scholarly outlets, including the yearly publications of the prestigious Texas Folklore Society. She continued to write sketches, short stories, and poems during the 1950s.[46]

Activists also contributed to the literature issued during the period. J. T. Canales, the former legislator from Brownsville, authored several essays between 1930 and 1945 on behalf of civil rights causes, then in 1945 reminisced in "Personal Recollections of J. T. Canales." He produced other historical pieces after 1945, among them *Bits of Texas History in the Melting Pot of America* (2 vols; Brownsville: privately printed, 1950, 1957) as well as titles on his kin Juan Cortina, among them *Juan N. Cortina Presents His Motion for a New Trial* (San Antonio: Artes Gráficas, 1951).[47] Alonso Perales, the LULAC activist, published *El méxico americano y la política de sur de Tejas* (San Antonio: Artes Gráficas, 1931) and *En defensa de mi raza* (San Antonio: Artes Gráficas, 1936 and 1937) to highlight the political disadvantages of Tejanos in South Texas.[48] In 1948, he compiled a volume of statements on discrimination and published them in *Are We Good Neighbors?* (San Antonio: Artes Gráficas, 1948).

The End of an Era

From 1945 to 1960, Texas Mexicans continued to experience oppression and exploitation, most severely in the rural regions in which racial attitudes relegated Tejanos to a second-class status.[49] But circumstances in the late 1950s for Texas Mexicans no longer resembled those of the 1940s. Within the community, for one, improved familiarity with American mainstream life offered more promise. While Tejano society had command of the Spanish language, observed Mexico's national holidays, and enjoyed Mexican music and other traditions of the motherland, a number of factors strengthened their attachment to United States institutions: World War II had acquainted Tejano veterans with an Anglo-American world they had previously known only vicariously; the G.I. Bill of Rights had proved instrumental in the education of many ex-servicemen, compulsory-school attendance laws came to be more strictly enforced, and the consumer culture of the era seduced the multitudes, many of whom had been United States born and knew no other than American life. Continued cultural syncretization improved Tejanos' chances to capitalize on the age's new opportunities.[50]

Meanwhile, de facto Jim Crow traditions for Texas Mexicans in the urban areas faced new threats due to the increasing influence of Mexican-American leaders and their sympathizers in the NAACP and labor unions as well as to initiatives undertaken by government and the courts to integrate public education and juries. By the late 1950s, political circumstances themselves conspired to weaken racism against Tejanos. The liberal wing of the Democratic party experienced a resurgence, and members of the Congress such as Lyndon Baines Johnson and Ralph Yarborough did not look upon Jim Crow as an appropriate system for the modern age. In Austin, legislators such as Henry B. González and Abraham Kazen initiated campaigns to overturn segregation.[51] As the decade closed, however, much remained to be accomplished in the struggle for equality. The 1960s and 1970s would see newer approaches in the campaign to achieve those ends.

The Sixties and El Movimiento
1960–1976

THE 1970 federal census estimated the Mexican-American population in Texas at approximately 2 million, a figure that represented about 20 percent of the state's entire population.[1] By that time, Tejanos could be found just about everywhere but principally in the agricultural counties of South Texas, the cattle- and sheep-raising sections of West Texas, the towns of the South Plains such as Lubbock, Amarillo, and Hereford, the El Paso region, and the inner cities of metroplexes such as San Antonio, Houston, and Dallas.

Socioeconomic differentiation characterized the Tejano population more than ever. Some 60 to 70 percent of Mexican-American male workers in the state were solidly in unskilled and semiskilled blue-collar occupations (machinists, craftsmen, laborers, service, farm workers and farm managers, and other unspecified positions). The Tejano middle class, meantime, continued to expand to as much as 40 percent of the Tejano community. The census listed increased numbers of Mexican-American craftsmen, clerks, salespersons, managers, proprietors, and professionals.[2]

Politics in the 1960s

In the early 1960s, many veteran activists began subscribing to political notions that parted from the moderate approaches to change that had characterized the postwar era. Several factors explain the turn. By the

1960s, new horizons seemed attainable for Texas Mexicans. The matter of race was no longer a major issue, and many of the barriers and obstacles against which the LULACers and G.I. Forumeers had fought since their organizations' inception had tumbled, among them school segregation, discouragement from jury service, and even the poll tax, which was barred by the 24th Amendment to the United States Constitution in 1964. Legislative and judicial intervention in the 1960s and 1970s, moreover, removed numerous handicaps that had restricted political participation. In 1962, the United States Supreme Court declared the principle of one man, one vote, thereby strengthening Texas-Mexican political representation. The federal Voting Rights Act of 1965 ensured fair elections at the local level. In 1969, the Texas legislature repealed the segregationist laws passed by that body in 1956–1957.³ With many old issues settled, Tejano activists took on newer causes.

Numerous problems lingered on as part of an entrenched past. Though the times were accepting of change, Anglo Texans remained temperamentally conservative and cautious especially in many rural regions in their concessions to what they still considered an inferior people. Discrimination seemed different only in its newfound subtlety; standard practices of segregation in residential areas, schools, and hiring practices died hard. Tejanos still stood in fear of the Texas Rangers, the Border Patrol, and even the local Sheriff's Department, remembering the long history of mistreatment at the hands of the these police bodies. Poverty stalked the great majority. Especially afflicted were *campesinos* (farm workers) who toiled in the fields with practically no help from an insensitive government. In both rural and urban areas, many parents were forced to keep their children from schools and send them instead to work in order to help meet the tight family budget. Education for Tejanos, in fact, was still in a shameful condition: Mexican schools remained segregated and underfinanced and many times under the tutelage of racist mentors. The resentment and frustration that these problems caused in part gave impetus to the new brand of Mexican-American politics of the 1960s and 1970s.

An early manifestation of the 1960s politics was Henry B. González's effort in 1958 to gain the Texas governor's seat. A San Antonio native, González had, during his term in the Texas senate in the 1950s, taken on struggles against Jim Crow, and González's quest for the governor's mansion had attracted political organizers of the era, primarily those who were working with the G.I. Forum and LULAC. González's run proved abortive (his record of attaining the most votes by a Mexican-American gubernatorial candidate remains unequalled), but the campaign nonetheless had inspired supporters to take on new battles.[4] In 1961, González went on to win election to the United States House of Representatives in a newly formed district that embraced most of Bexar County's Mexican barrios. In 1964, Eligio "Kika" de la Garza of South Texas joined González in the House.[5]

Then in 1961, Mexican-American organizers who had helped John F. Kennedy win the presidency through "Viva Kennedy" Clubs established the Political Association of Spanish-speaking Organizations (PASO). Indignant at what seemed a lack of progress for Mexican Americans, PASO challenged the credibility of Anglos and the old Mexican-American leadership and encouraged more community involvement. By the mid–1960s, this political organization had extended its denunciations to all levels of government, blaming local and federal authorities for the impoverishment of Tejanos. Though such criticism appeared much more severe than the politics of the Mexican-American Generation, the fact of the matter was that PASO in the early 1960s represented a blend of liberal and moderate positions.[6]

By the tumultuous 1960s, then, Tejano middle-class leaders had prepared to join the ranks of liberal politicians and call for increased action on the part of government. Protest movements at the national level for civil rights, gay liberation, equality for women, and against the war in Vietnam incited bolder action. Mexican Americans themselves drew inspiration during the mid–1960s from unionizing efforts in California led by a labor activist named César Chávez. In June 1967, Reies López Tijerina launched a highly publicized campaign to regain land grants previously owned by Mexican Americans in New Mexico. In Texas proper, in 1963, PASO and the Teamsters union masterminded a political upset in Crystal City, helping to elect an all-Mexican ticket to the city council. Then, strike activity among the campesinos in South Texas farms and a subsequent "Minimum Wage March" during the summer of 1966 fomented a broad movement calling the entire American political system into question.[7]

THE MINIMUM WAGE MARCH

In June 1966, Tejano farm workers struck and then walked from the Rio Grande Valley to Austin. Governor John Connally, who opposed receiving the protestors at the statehouse, met them at New Braunfels and rejected their plea for a special session of the legislature. Throngs of supporters, among them LULAC, the G.I. Forum, and PASO members accompanied the marchers into the capital. The 490-mile trek and the passion it created, together with the governor's crass conduct, brought together diverse sectors of the Texas-Mexican community.[8]

The result was what came to be known as the "Chicano Movement" (*"el movimiento"*), an expression of dissatisfaction that paralleled other outbursts of the era. Abruptly, segments of the Tejano population broke out in discontent, even as important advances in social relations were underway. Indeed, many of those who became leaders of the movimiento had reached maturity following Jim Crow's demise and had personally experienced only the vestiges of the vicious old-time racism. But the younger cohorts nonetheless felt frustration at the limits of ethnic advancement, and in common with other young people during the 1960s and 1970s, resented the pressure toward consensus, the emphasis on materialism, and the pattern of predictability in American society. The very power of Americanization that had historically produced moderate styles in Tejano politics now begot, at least temporarily, a confrontational approach toward dealing with problems long addressed by earlier reformist Tejanos. Enduring nationalist sentiments influenced the political and cultural dimensions of *la causa* (the cause).

The Middle Class and the Movement

In truth, the Movement consisted of an admixture of moderate and militant thinking. Within the ranks of LULAC and the G.I. Forum, exasperation had prevailed over the neglect of the Mexican-American population in the Johnson administration's Great Society programs. To mollify his critics, President Johnson scheduled cabinet committee hearings on Mexican-American affairs to be held in El Paso, Texas, in October 1967. Because the list of participants omitted the emerging leaders of the era such as Chávez, Tijerina, and Rodolfo "Corky" González of Colorado, some of the delegates chose instead to attend a rump convention organized in the city's barrios. The delegates to what became known as the Raza Unida Conference tended to be combative in their criticism of white society and their discourse tended to exalt the superiority of Mexican-American life over that of Anglo-American culture.[9]

As part of the "Chicano Movement," older groups such as LULAC and the G. I. Forum tapped their connections to Washington; among programs that these organizations enacted in the mid–1960s with millions of federal dollars was a job training and placement project for the unemployed poor called the Service, Employment, and Redevelopment Agency (SER).[10] Simultaneously, middle-class activists took an interest in Mexican-American political campaigns as well as in school walkouts and different forms of public demonstration that were being led by the more feisty elements within the Movement. PASO, for its part, took notice of these forms of protest but focused its energies more on political activities that had prospects of getting the candidates they endorsed, regardless of race, into office and thereby help Mexican Americans. By the late 1960s, however, PASO yielded to the more militant strain of the Movement as its middle-class philosophy acted to put distance between itself and a community that was becoming more receptive to militant politics. Thus, it lost the chance to lead an important movement which in some ways it had set forth.[11]

But newer middle-class organizations also surfaced out of the movimiento, among them the Mexican American Legal Defense and Education Fund (MALDEF), founded in 1968. Funded by government grants and private corporations, MALDEF worked through the courts to protect Mexican-American rights. It assailed, for instance, those practices which marred equal educational opportunities, such as discriminatory school funding or continued segregation. In so doing, it took several cases into the courts, among the most famous being *Cisneros* v. *Corpus Christi Independent School District* (1970).[12]

As schools officials utilized the accepted Mexican-American classification of "white" as a subterfuge in school desegregation and continued the pattern of excluding Mexican Americans from Anglos' schools, lawyers for Mexican Americans moved away from the old claim that Mexican Americans were white people. Attorneys adopted the position that Mexican Americans must be recognized as an "identifiable ethnic group." This new categorization would circumvent the ploy used by Anglo-controlled school boards of using Tejanos (classified as white) to integrate the schools. The Mexican-American community was gratified when in June 1970, a federal district judge ruled that Mexican Americans could be considered an identifiable ethnic minority and that the equal protection of the law under the Fourteenth Amendment applied to them. Though the case was appealed, in 1973 the United States Supreme Court acknowledged the separate legal status of Mexican Americans. For MALDEF, the decision provided an important legal mechanism for its desegregation cases.[13]

Middle-class organizations such as LULAC, the G.I. Forum, and MALDEF had always made education one of their priorities, and they heeded complaints by students who grieved that school systems treated them unfairly in many ways. Principals and teachers, they protested, criticized their heritage, editorialized about politics and the negative role of Mexican Americans in history, enforced a "no Spanish" rule, discouraged them from involvement in certain school functions, neglected their needs when it came to charting out career plans, and overlooked Mexican-American applicants when hiring teachers and administrators who might have acted as positive role models. By the mid–1970s, however, school districts had conceded many of these demands.

Of all reforms, however, Mexican Americans were most adamant about bilingual education, a program enacted by Congress in 1967 to alleviate the educational problems Mexican-American students faced. Bilingual education seemed to give students a sense of self-esteem and facilitated teaching, at least according to national studies that argued that instruction in a native language enhanced the learning process. Further, it circumvented the "no Spanish" rule and permitted a positive interpretation of Mexican Americans' role in history. Moreover, necessary modifications made in the curriculum would attend to particular needs of Mexican Americans. But despite its merits, Mexican Americans failed to pass the legislation that would have implemented a strong program of bilingual education during the late 1960s and early 1970s. State Representative Carlos Truán (Democrat-Corpus Christi) did succeed in having a bilingual education act passed in 1969, but the law only asked local districts to voluntarily begin the program. Without state and judicial support, such efforts did not fare well.[14]

El Movimiento "Chicano"

MEXICAN AMERICAN YOUTH ORGANIZATION

The events of 1966 and 1967 set in motion another struggle, more militant in style, headed by the Mexican American Youth Organization. Formally organized in 1967 by José Angel Gutiérrez and four others,

MAYO sought to act upon long-standing problems confronting Mexican Americans, among them segregation, harassment from law-enforcement authorities, and inferior schooling. MAYO activists took example from the militant style of African-American radicals and copied the example of the striking campesinos in California who had turned to the heritage of the pre-Columbian peoples of Mexico for cultural symbols and heroes. Many MAYO activists were students recruited from colleges, but their ties were to the grassroots, the segment of the Tejano community that MAYO purported to represent.[15]

This MAYO-influenced strain of the Movement adopted the self-referent term "Chicano" as suggestive of the resurgent cultural awareness. Chicanos rediscovered their Aztec and Mayan heritage and proclaimed it chauvinistically. Like some Anglo counterparts, they grew long hair and beards, and adopted the defiant Hippie garb of the period. In their politics, the militants damned mainstream society for the long history of oppression and criticized middle-class leaders as sellouts to *la raza* (the Mexican American people).[16] Beatings of Mexican Americans at the hands of policemen, alleged injustices inflicted by school administrators upon Chicano students, and electoral machination were cases that activists cited when publicizing their cause, thus winning new adherents to their columns. School boycotts also became a strategy for making the educational system responsive to Mexican Americans, and student walkouts were initiated in numerous towns from the Texas Panhandle to the greater border region in the period between the late 1960s and early 1970s.[17]

CRYSTAL CITY

Meanwhile, another activist group, La Raza Unida party (RUP) guided the militancy of the era, according to Ignacio García, one of the most knowledgeable students of the party. RUP's earliest victories came in 1970 in Crystal City, Texas, the small rural town in Zavala County which had been the setting for the aforementioned state victory in 1963. It also happened to be the hometown of José Ángel Gutiérrez, one of MAYO's founders. When Gutiérrez returned to *Cristal* (as it is known in Spanish) in the spring of 1969, he organized Mexican-American high-school students who were at that time in a state of complete discontent over the preferential treatment that school accorded the Anglo student minority.[18]

Things came to a head in October 1969 when the Crystal City High School Ex-Students Association proposed that it be permitted to select a queen and her entourage for the approaching homecoming game. But it was a school requirement that all candidates for homecoming queen have a father or mother who had received a degree from their town's high school, a criterion which severely limited the pool of Mexican-American prospects. When the angry students and their parents, organized by Gutiérrez and his wife Luz, failed to persuade the school board to reject the Ex-Students Association's petition to use the school campus for their activities, the young people walked out of classes on December 9, 1969.

For almost a month, through the Christmas holidays, the boycott remained in place, reaching a high of 65 percent total student absenteeism. As funds figured on attendance, the school system suffered gravely, so during the first week of January 1970, the board arranged a truce with the students, acquiescing to many of their requests. The protestors then lifted the boycott.[19]

RAZA UNIDA PARTY

Spinning off the confrontation was *Ciudadanos Unidos* (United Citizens), a political alliance founded by the parents of the boycotters and other sympathizers who sought to sustain the political momentum in Cristal following the resolution of the school issue. In the spring 1970 city and school board elections Gutiérrez turned to Ciudadanos Unidos to help them contest Anglo electoral dominance of the town.[20]

In January 1970, Ciudadanos Unidos created the Raza Unida party, whose antecedents harked back to 1967 when MAYO sponsored several Raza Unida unity conferences at which leaders from different parts of the nation encouraged young people and prospective followers to get involved in the Chicano movement; the organizational meeting of the Raza Unida conference, of course, had been held in El Paso in that same year. Now, as Crystal City students boycotted in December 1969, MAYO met in Mission, Texas, and called for the formation of a third political party. Following RUP's founding, MAYO people directed their priorities to politics, and as a consequence their organization began to fade. By 1971, RUP supplanted MAYO as the main force of Chicano political organizing in Texas.[21]

In the 1970 elections, the slate Gutiérrez assembled took posts on the

Crystal City school board and city council and soon gained dominance of both. Numerous reforms followed. In the schools, the new officers enacted bilingual instruction, developed Chicano history courses, established a free lunch program, and hired Mexican-American personnel to replace teachers who found the new environment uncomfortable. At the city level, the party replaced Anglos with Raza Unida people and aggressively pursued federal monies. The Chicano "takeover" of the town gained widespread notice, inasmuch as it symbolized what Chicanos in other parts of the country could achieve with commitment and sound organization.[22]

Confident that the Crystal City success story could be duplicated elsewhere, RUP supporters from throughout the state gathered in San Antonio on October 31, 1971, to contemplate RUP's direction. Delegates decided to establish RUP as a statewide party that would run candidates in the 1972 elections.[23]

Most visible of the RUP candidates in 1972 was its nominee for governor, Ramsey Muñiz, a Corpus Christi native who held a law degree from Baylor University and who, at the time of his selection for the governor's position, was a MAYO organizer in the Waco area. As the RUP candidate, he spoke for a leftist-liberal platform which the party had hammered out in June 1972. The plank stressed education, calling on schools to implement programs which would meet Mexican-American needs and demanding that the state's school funding be dispersed more fairly. It called on government to partition cities into districts so that barrios would be equally represented in ruling bodies. Among other things, the RUP platform addressed foreign policy, health, and the standard of living. It supported ratification of the Equal Rights Amendment and demanded that the Texas Rangers be disbanded. When the ballots were counted, Muñiz received 6.28 percent of the vote to the Democrat's 47.8 percent and the Republicans 45.08 percent. By drawing votes away from the Democrats, RUP made the major parties recognize it as a formidable alternative in Texas politics.[24]

From the period between 1970 and 1973, RUP came to claim several victories throughout several South Texas towns. RUP-backed candidates in Cotulla (La Salle County) and RUP sympathizers in Carrizo Springs (Dimmit County) won in 1970, the same time that Gutiérrez and his supporters had won in the Crystal City school board and city council. In Robstown (Nueces County), where a boycott of students in the schools brought in RUP activists in 1972, party members gained a place in the city government. In Kingsville (Kleberg County), RUP activities duplicated the Robstown feat. Pearsall, San Juan, and Edcouch-Elsa in the Lower Rio Grande Valley, and Eagle Pass, Kyle, San Marcos, Lockhart, Hebbronville, Beeville, and even smaller communities in Far West Texas's Brewster and El Paso counties were among the other places in which RUP or its sympathizers won local offices during the early 1970s.[25]

WOMEN IN THE MOVEMENT

Throughout Texas, women played significant roles in the movimiento. Women had been part of the Movement since its beginnings; their ranks came from veteran activists such as Virginia Músquiz, believed to be the first Mexican-American woman to run for the state legislature (1964) and a participant in the Crystal City movimiento in 1969, as well as María L. Hernández, founder of the Orden Caballeros de America in 1929, who campaigned for RUP candidates in the early 1970s.[26] The greater number of women activists, however, were college students who had joined MAYO in the late 1960s. Following the founding of RUP, some women won political office under the RUP banner and others played prominent roles as members of the party's leadership.[27]

Women's part in the movimiento, however, was not limited to politics, as many advocated feminism and urged assertiveness for women. Leaders directed themselves toward the amelioration of such problems as poor educational standings, discriminatory wage structures, the right of women to control of their own bodies, and family care. To address these issues, Tejanas convened in Houston in May 1971 in what is considered to be the first national conference ever organized to specifically deal with Mexican-American women's concerns. This *Conferencia de Mujeres por la Raza* (National Chicana Conference) was attended by hundreds of women from diverse sections of the country.

Middle-class Mexican-American women advocated similar goals. LULAC's Women's Affairs Committee held its first state convention in Houston in November 1972, and approximately 250 women attended from Texas and elsewhere. They passed resolutions encouraging LULAC to work for more significant government appointments for women. They resolved to reform the prevailing role of the Mexican-

American woman as a homemaker and to inspire women to assume a more visible role in society and political affairs.[28]

DECLINE OF EL MOVIMIENTO

By the mid–1970s, the movimiento faced a downturn, as attested to by RUP's inability to follow up on earlier gains. Political victories were limited to Crystal City and Cotulla in the spring of 1974, and in Cristal, divisiveness now smoldered as two factions of RUP vied for the same offices. The new group accused the Gutiérrez-led party of seeking self-aggrandizement and being despotic. Then, Ramsey Muñiz's second run at the gubernatorial office in November 1974 proved to be less significant than the first: the result prompting many to reassess the prospects of the party at the state level. In Cristal, Gutiérrez did win the position of County Judge in 1974, and RUP won other county offices. But Gutiérrez's talk about getting Anglo ranchers to pay more taxes on their lands and the rise of a new faction in Cristal that challenged Gutiérrez on ideological grounds did not bode well for effective rule from Raza Unida.[29]

Numerous factors conspired to exhaust the movimiento. Ideological splits hurt. The difficulty of fundraising constrained the party's ability to wage effective campaigns. Harassment of RUP organizers by Texas Rangers, legal attacks, and sub rosa efforts designed to cast a shady image on activists made RUP people fearful. The defeat of the Gutiérristas in Crystal City in April 1976 by the opposition RUP faction (with some support from Anglo Democrats) did not help the Movement. Then, the power of Texas governor Dolph Briscoe came down hard on Gutiérrez's plan to establish a collective farm in Zavala County. Calling it an effort to establish a "little Cuba" in Texas, the governor succeeded in lobbying against a $1.5 million federal grant to be used in funding the project and caused voters to regard the RUP experiment as socialism.[30]

In the end, the changing times made the movimiento seem anachronistic. Its militant rhetoric and tactics seemed passé. Many of the Movement's aims became institutionalized as well. In the gubernatorial election of November 1978, RUP did not garner the necessary 2 percent vote to remain viable for subsequent elections, and with that exhibition went its fate as a third party force.[31] In 1980, Gutiérrez himself was forced to resign his position as the Zavala County judge.

LEGACY OF EL MOVIMIENTO

Still the movimiento left an enduring mark. Women activists had modified old sexual stereotypes and earned concessions on equality, thereby improving Mexican-American women's hopes for a better education, possible professional careers, and to have real input in decisions about the size and management of the family. Also, RUP wrested power from Anglos in the Democratic party, most visibly in South Texas, for as RUP declined, ex-members joined the Mexican American Democrats (MAD—founded in late 1976) and moved in to the fill openings created by RUP's void. Then, the Movement invigorated the reform organizations of the pre-Movement era like LULAC and the G.I. Forum. Some of their veterans became MAD members also while others participated in the Southwest Voter Registration Education Project (1974), founded by Willie Velásquez.[32] The Movement also motivated many to work on behalf of the less advantaged, among them the campesinos, juvenile delinquents, and poverty-stricken families. The movimiento's emphasis on cultural pride led student activists to strive for the establishment of Chicano studies (classes in high schools and even departments in universities), while faculty and students together developed classes in a variety of subjects salient to Chicanos. A Chicano literary renaissance occurred which led to new activities in music, theatre, creative writing, and scholarship. The fiction works of Tejano authors such as Tomás Rivera, Ricardo Sánchez, and Rolando Hinojosa-Smith won international acclaim. Chicano scholarly studies commenced finding their way into professional journals, many of them revising the old image of Chicanos as a quaint people who were a burden to society.[33] Old publications on Mexican Americans were reread, among them those of Dr. George I. Sánchez and Dr. Américo Paredes, both of the University of Texas.

Labor Unionism in the Cities and on the Farms

Though the post–World War II decline in labor activism continued into the 1960s and 1970s, Mexican Americans still strove to improve their working conditions, primarily by allying themselves with unions. In El Paso, Mexican-American women joined the Amalgamated Clothing Workers of America (ACWA) and in 1972 struck several Farah Manufacturing Company plants, one of the major employers in the city. The garment workers (primarily Mexican immigrants and Mexican Americans) sought protection from low wages, dangerous health and safety conditions, the presence of harassing and racist supervisors, and other types of mistreatment.

The strike in El Paso intensified to the level of a national boycott of Farah products. Ultimately, the tactic forced Farah to shut down some of its plants in Texas and New Mexico and, in March 1974, to accept the ACWA as the union representing Farah workers. The strikers were not completely pleased with their new contract but felt that at least they had won union protection.

In the mid–1970s, Farah's fortunes continued on the downswing due to the recession in 1974–1975, adverse publicity generated by the way its management had dealt with the strike, and poor executive-level decisions made in production and marketing. To keep going, the company released several workers and intimidated union leaders. Such a tenuous situation forced workers in 1977 to make numerous concessions to management in order to keep the factory afloat and thus save their jobs.[34]

Another major strike involving Tejanos during the 1960s and 1970s was that of the aforementioned farm workers whose minimum wage march in the summer of 1966 is credited with kindling the Chicano Movement in Texas. Actually, the campesinos had profited little from the famed pilgrimage: in the 1970s, they still faced lamentable working conditions. Most fields lacked restrooms, and since modesty compelled women to delay their bodily functions for hours, they suffered from disproportionally high levels of kidney infections. Wages remained as low as $2 or $3 for a typical day of field labor. Diseases such as typhoid, typhus, dysentery, and leprosy afflicted farm workers to a degree unknown to other Texans. Infant morality rates among the campesinos in South Texas were among the highest in the United States at the time, and the life expectancy for field hands hovered around forty-nine years. Farm workers did not enjoy basic benefits from state laws, such as the right to collective bargaining, workman's compensation, and unemployment benefits.[35]

To assist the Texas campesinos following the March of 1966, César Chávez had sent Antonio Orendain from California to Texas to take charge of a small chapter of Chávez's own fledgling United Farm Workers' Union (UFWU). But resistance to union activity in Texas was fierce, and strikes were easy to break with scabs from across the border. Fearing violence and wishing to focus his efforts on unionizing in California, Chávez recalled Orendain in 1967, and the UFWU chapter in Texas declined.[36]

Two years later, Orendain returned to the Rio Grande Valley and for a period undertook aggressive organizing efforts. In 1975, however, Chávez fired his UFWU lieutenant for leading strike activities at a time during which Chávez was negotiating important labor contracts in California and could have done better without the new controversy. In response, Orendain formed the independent Texas Farm Workers Union (TFWU). By the mid–1970s, thus, two Texas farm workers' unions sought different strategies in efforts to improve the lot of the campesinos.[37]

Toward the Age of "Hispanics"

For a ten-year period following the Farm Workers March of 1966, a general regard for the good of la raza had held together a cause marked by differences in class lines, generations, and ideologies. During the era, Texas Mexicans had pursued political tactics previously shunned by activists of the Mexican-American Generation and could claim, by the mid–1970s, to have made strides that had built upon their predecessors' accomplishments. When it was spent, the Chicano Movement left important statements, not the least of which was the pledge that Tejanos would no longer accede to labels of submissiveness and inferiority.

Indeed, Anglo Americans came to reject the notion that Texas Mexicans were to be kept on society's periphery as had been the case during previous generations. Privately, Anglos still harbored contempt for "Meskins" and worked surreptitiously to retard their progress, but now Anglos accepted the fact that the majority of Tejanos could translate their numbers into economic and political clout. Businessmen, therefore, moved away from gestures that might alienate Texas-Mexican customers. Politicians stopped discounting the Mexican-American presence and became aware of the potential of a mobilized Tejano electorate. In the 1980s, then, Texas Mexicans would face a racial structure more receptive to their contributions.

CHAPTER TEN

Hispanic Texans
1976 to the Present

As of 1990, the Texas-Mexican population stood just above 4 million.[1] This figure, of course, was an undercount, for census takers have never fully succeeded in counting those who come to Texas from Mexico illegally. Of the estimate given by the 1980 census, slightly over 80 percent were Mexican Americans—that is, they were native born. An overwhelming majority—some 86.1 percent of the total population—lived in urbanized areas.[2]

The Middle Class and the Marginalized Masses

Significant disparities in standards of living stamped the Tejano community during the years of the late 1970s and 1980s. On the one hand, there existed the poorest of people living in makeshift homes in unincorporated subdivisions (*colonias*) along the border; there living conditions matched the worst kind of circumstances Tejanos had ever faced. The fact of the matter was that some 20 percent of Tejano families lived in impoverished circumstances in the Lone Star State, and the future did not look bright for them.[3]

At the upper extreme were more fortunate folks belonging to the old middle class but also those tracing their well-being to the Great Society initiatives of the 1960s as well as the Chicano Movement: these two spells of liberalism had produced increased student enrollment at the levels of higher education and newer opportunities in the business world. Overtures by government and the private sector to the formerly neglected Hispanic voter and consumer led to the further incorporation of upwardly mobile Mexican Americans into the state's government bureaucracy and corporate structure.[4]

Thus, the internal fragmentation perceptible in the Tejano community since the eighteenth century remained, now in the form of a prominent middle class sector and a broader community constituted of the impoverished masses. As the Tejano community entered the twenty-first century, the former group appeared integrated into the mainstream. At the bottom languished the economically disadvantaged and marginalized multitudes.

A Moderate Political Age

Following the Chicano Movement, Texas Mexicans adjusted to a political climate similar to that which prevailed during the 1940s and 1950s when only socially sanctioned challenges to the status quo were condoned. During this post–1970s period of moderation, the designation "Hispanic" became acceptable as a label that symbolized a realignment in political directions. While acting as an all-embracing term for those having cultural roots in the Latin American countries, the word presumed decreasing identification with ethnicity but a continued acknowledgment of being Mexican American.[5] Corporations and departments of government which in the 1970s directed themselves at the expanding Mexican-American middle class popularized the use of the term "Hispanic." The term won acceptance among those who had disapproved of the militancy of the 1960s and 1970s and rejected such terms as "Chicano," by Tejano businessmen who found new opportunities in the 1970s and 1980s and sought to appeal to a wider spectrum of the buying public, and by activists who found it a neutral label in formal commentary.[6]

In the cautious politics of the post-Movement era, the middle class maintained its role as political arbiter and spokesman for the Mexican-American electorate. As indicated, the Chicano Movement had included middle-class partisans, and as the organizations of the 1960s and 1970s waned, this element moved in to seize opportunities available within the Democratic party. The middle-class reformist groups of old similarly profited from the movimiento. LULAC, for one, recaptured its place as the most-noted organization, and along with MALDEF assumed a major function in acting as intermediary between Mexican Americans and officialdom.[7]

In pursuit of a moderate agenda, LULAC departed from the high-profile politics espoused by LULAC National President Ruben Bonilla in the late 1970s and early 1980s. According to Bonilla, LULACers afraid of jeopardizing their connections to Washington, D.C., had foiled his efforts to take LULAC in a more liberal direction, such as reproaching the stand that the country had taken on immigration from Mexico or criticizing U.S. political involvement in Latin America. MALDEF softened its rebuke of white society, for as it lost its federal funding in the 1980s, it turned to the conservative corporate sector for support. Neither organization, of course, became reactionary, but certainly they both assumed a more centrist disposition.[8]

Also reflecting the trend toward moderation in the 1980s was the election of neoliberal Tejano leaders to office. The most visible of these political figures was Henry Cisneros (Mayor, San Antonio) who, along with others in Colorado and California, voiced Mexican-American interests and advocated politics that were more redolent of the pre–World War II era than those of the Chicano Movement. Though Cisneros did not reject his Mexican Americanness, he did not make ethnicity a political issue, and his critics faulted him for lacking a specific agenda for Mexican Americans.[9]

IMPROVED POLITICAL STANDING

At a time of moderate politics, thus, Tejanos witnessed numerous advances in political representation. Actually, such gains resulted from changes generated by forces emanating from previous historical epochs. In the 1960s and 1970s, government had taken the lead in efforts to coerce society to change its biases against racial minorities, a public consensus built up to combat the blatant racism of the pre–1960s era, and the Chicano Movement had opened doors to the incorporation of Tejanos into the political and economic mainstream.[10]

In 1984, Raúl A. González was appointed to the Texas Supreme Court by the governor and went on to win election in his own right. In 1990, Dan Morales won office as the first Hispanic Attorney General of Texas. According to the Texas Almanac, the number of Spanish-surnamed senators and representatives in the state legislature increased from about fifteen to twenty-three between 1976 and 1991. Among those listed in 1990 were Irma Rangel and Lena Guerrero (who in 1991 was appointed to head the Texas Railroad Commission by the governor). The number of Spanish-surnamed county commissioners and county judges rose from approximately 70 in 1976 to 107 in 1990.[11] In San Antonio, locally educated Henry Cisneros, a graduate of George Washington University with a doctorate in public administration, won the mayor's seat in 1981, the first Mexican American to do so since Juan Seguín during the days of the Texas Republic. The border counties of South Texas finally yielded to the political control of the Mexican-American majority.[12] In numerous Texas cities, including the metroplexes, there was Tejano representation in lower-level courts, the constabulary, city councils, school boards, as well as in nonelective positions with political influence. In the United States House of Representatives, four Mexican Americans were serving during the early 1990s, including old warriors such as Henry B. González of San Antonio and Eligio "Kika" de la Garza from the Rio Grande Valley. From 1977 to 1979, Leonel Castillo of Houston became head of the Immigration and Naturalization Service during the presidency of Jimmy Carter. In 1988, Lauro Cavazos, who was born on the King Ranch, was appointed Secretary of Education and served until late 1990.

Increased electoral influence was evident in other ways. For example, Mexican-American votes contributed to the election of populist Anglo Americans at the state level. Ballot power also influenced the passage of several bills designed to bring about school-finance reform, to improve the lot of the campesinos, and provide health assistance to the poor.[13]

Despite their many accomplishments, Texas Mexicans remained a long way from achieving political equity. Though Texas exceeded other states in the number of elected Mexican-American officeholders, those numbers were deceiving, as Texas Mexicans constituted 20 percent of the state's total population yet claimed only a little over 5 percent representation in city councils and approximately 6 percent on school boards.[14]

The same circumstances that produced political moderation, moreover, dampened possibilities for future gains, and so Texas-Mexican politicians remained committed to the cause of the masses. Those in the forefront of this mission came from segments of the middle class who still subscribed to a long-standing regard for *la gente* (the people). But often, their attempts to help the impoverished were frustrated by the very institutions for which they worked, as their concern over job security discouraged them from being too aggressive in their commitment to social change. In the assessment of the historian Rodolfo Acuña, this cohort acted as brokers who served the good of ruling interests instead of the Texas-Mexican community.[15]

The Ethnic Agenda

As spokespersons, Tejano leaders addressed ethnic policies but also other issues that affected Mexican Americans as lower-class folks. Among those speaking for ethnic causes was Willie Velásquez (one of the founders of MAYO) who established the Southwest Voter Registration Education Project (SVREP) in San Antonio in 1974 for the purpose of registering more Mexican-American voters throughout the United States and eliminating institutional obstacles to political power. While SVREP sought to get out the Hispanic vote and see Mexican Americans elected, it joined MALDEF and other groups to overturn laws (such as those dealing with at-large elections) that deterred Mexican Americans from equal representation and that weakened Tejano political clout.[16] Also committed to the goal of Mexican-American equality was Raúl Yzaguirre of Texas, who since 1974 had headed the National Council of La Raza, a Washington, D.C., public advocacy group founded in 1968.[17]

BETTER EDUCATION

Mexican Americans also carried on their crusade for better education, though after the mid–1970s, for several reasons, they deemphasized integration. Anglos resisted court-mandated desegregation strenuously, and school districts usually found ways to delay it. More significantly, desegregation plans usually favored Anglos instead of Mexican Americans: it was the latter who were usually bused out of their district to comply with integration orders, for example. As time passed, therefore, support for desegregation as a way to educational parity declined among Mexican Americans. According to Guadalupe San Miguel, parents and Mexican-American educators now turned to bilingual programs for education remedies.[18]

Despite unremitting attempts to create an effective bilingual program, Mexican-American educators in Texas in the mid–1970s still had only a weak law mandating bilingual education from kindergarten through the third grade. In the face of this failure to enact a more effective program, bilingual education activists turned to the courts, arguing that the status quo deprived Mexican-American students of a sound education. In the legislature, Carlos Truán, whose battles for bilingual education originated in the late 1960s, continued his commitment but met little success, as public opinion opposed this compensatory program and a spate of reports from the government and private institutes argued that such approaches were expensive, ineffectual, and potentially divisive.[19]

But then in January 1981, Judge William Wayne Justice ruled that the state bilingual education plan was unacceptable to the court and ordered immediate reform. Armed with this opinion, Truán in May 1981 introduced a new bill which would establish the bilingual program in schools through the sixth grade where districts had at least twenty school children with only a rudimentary command of the English language. Again, Truán faced resistance, but his argument for a bill that would help the state avoid Judge Justice's more extreme solution to the system's shortcomings swayed his adversaries. Thus had Truán and his supporters succeeded in acquiring a stronger program despite the power of the opposition. The immediate impetus had been Judge Justice's decision.[20]

On another front, Mexican Americans with the assistance of MALDEF questioned the institutionalized method of dispersing funds to the public school system, reasoning that it discriminated against students residing in school districts with lower tax bases. In 1968, parents of Mexican-American school children enrolled at the financially distressed Edgewood Independent School district in San Antonio brought suit against the state in *Rodríguez* v. *San Antonio Independent School District*. The case had gone to the United States Supreme Court which ruled in 1973 for the reconsideration of the existing school finance formula. But the justices deferred to the state legislators and left it to them to resolve the matter.[21]

In 1984, MALDEF once again helped file suit, but this time in state court. In *Edgewood Independent School District* v. *Kirby*, the Texas Supreme Court ruled in October 1989 that the system of school financing violated the Texas constitution and that an equitable system of school financing be produced by the state legislature. In the spring of 1990, after several special sessions, state lawmakers approved a $528 million school finance compromise to take effect in the fall of that year.[22] But as of the early 1990s, the issue had not reached final resolution.

THE PLIGHT OF THE FARM WORKERS

Another issue of priority for Texas-Mexican leaders, especially those from South Texas, was the plight of farm workers. For the decade following Tony Orendain's split with Chávez in 1975, the TFWU and the California-based United Farm Workers (by now an AFL-CIO affiliate) vied to speak for an estimated 170,000 campesinos who worked the Texas fields.[23] Facing continued failures in the Texas legislature for collective bargaining rights, Orendain's more publicity-oriented TFWU staged dramatic marches: one in 1977 to Washington, D.C., in what proved to be a failed visit with President Jimmy Carter; the second in 1979 from Muleshoe in the Texas Panhandle to Austin. The most intensive efforts by Orendain and by Rebecca Flores Harrington, the state director of the UFW since 1975, were of lobbying state legislators, however, as each realized that without a labor law mandating union elections, agribusiness management could easily replace strikers with scabs.[24] In the early 1980s, however, the independent TFWU began to lose strength. Representation of farm workers' needs then fell to Flores Harrington, her husband James C. Harrington, attorney for the UFW, and the rank-and-file workers who constituted the many organizing committees throughout South Texas.[25]

In 1981, Mexican-American legislators from the trans-Nueces introduced an array of bills designed to win farm workers' unemployment compensation, workers' compensation in case of injury on the job, and collective bargaining rights. Other prospective bills would prohibit work with *el cortito*, or the short-handled hoe which caused disabling back illnesses in stoop laborers, and an end to child labor when students were supposed to be in school. The latter two became laws in 1981 while the State Health Department that same year directed growers to make provisions for field rest rooms, handwashing facilities, and good drinking water for the workers. Then, a favorable court ruling led to the enactment of a workers' compensation law in 1984 and an unemployment compensation act in 1985.[26] In 1987, the Texas legislature passed a law requiring that laborers be informed of any pesticides that may have been sprayed on the crops that they were working, and another one increasing the minimum wage from $1.40 to $3.35 an hour. During the late 1980s, Flores Harrington and UFW members also succeeded in negotiating contracts with some growers and establishing day-care centers in select South Texas colonias for the children of campesinos. Still remaining for the union to achieve was a collective bargaining law.[27]

But farm workers faced newer problems. Technology and mechanization seriously jeopardized the role of the field hand. Further, the agribusiness firms became increasingly reluctant to invest in Texas where winter freezes, even in South Texas, were too unpredictable. Instead, they sought to expand into Mexico and Central America.[28]

Aside from education and labor, other causes with specific relevance to Tejanos as a disadvantaged ethnic group attracted the concern of Mexican-American leaders. Anglo opposition to affirmative action still remained, and some now challenged the right of people to speak Spanish in public places—the so-called "English-Only" movement—in the mid–1980s. Racist feelings against Mexican Americans were expressed subtly in public alarms over being inundated by "illegal aliens."[29] Other expressions were not as implied: in the late 1970s a spate of killings of Mexican Americans in Houston, Castroville, Garden City, and other Texas cities at the hands of Anglo policemen caused Mexican-American protestors to raise the specter of racist motivation. As of the early 1990s, cries of police brutality still rang out.

Working-Class Interests

In recent times, middle-class advocates for the masses did not always strictly limit their attention to Mexican-American concerns. To the contrary, they dealt with matters that affected Tejanos as members of the poorer class. Since those issues transcended ethnicity, little effort was made to transform them into ethnic affairs.

For example, Communities Organized for Public Services (COPS) in San Antonio looked after the needs of the residents of the inner city (not necessarily Mexicans) who wished flood control, better street maintenance, and increased attention to housing. Parallel organizations that pursued related objectives existed in the Lower Rio Grande Valley and other Texas cities, among them El Paso where EPISO (El Paso In-

terreligious Sponsoring Organization) sought the political empowerment of Mexican Americans through the polling booth.[30] Elsewhere,
Mexican Americans entered into coalitions with other disadvantaged
groups to engineer better political redistricting. In Houston in 1978,
the Mexican-American leadership endorsed almost unanimously the establishment of the Metropolitan Transit Authority, a public bus-line
plan to replace the city's outmoded mass transit system.[31]

Epilogue

Heritage in part has shaped the course of Tejano history. Mexican
Americans in Texas have remained faithful to aspects of their Mexican
past, and they have preserved that linkage through the Spanish language, familial relationships, fiestas patrias commemorations, music
and other arts, and an assortment of retained cultural customs. This preserved ethnicity in turn has triggered intolerance and harsh negative
reactions from Anglo Texans.

On the other hand, the Tejano experience also resembles the classic
pattern of immigrant accommodation. Over the years Tejanos accepted
aspects of the dominant culture and ultimately penetrated previously
exclusive areas of Anglo power, including the white-collar professions
and politics.

The world of Tejanos is not one of two cultural polarities, however.
Though many of the struggles undertaken by Tejanos have been waged
as ethnic contests—among them the cause of civil rights, school discrimination, and labor oppression—they have been led by people who
were biethnic. Heritages have fused since 1836, so that Tejanos have
contributed to the Texas saga uniquely—drawing from two traditions
when presenting themselves before the schools, the workplace, the bureaucracy, the churches, and those institutions that deterred shared
aspirations.

The syncretization of cultures, however, has not produced a "typical
Tejano." Too many variables produced diversity, among them disparate
rates of assimilation, socioeconomic standing, mastery of the English
language (in the 1980 census, 6 percent of respondents noted that
Spanish was not a language used in the home), increased conversion to
Protestantism (5 percent adhered to Protestant beliefs in the 1980s),
and geographical setting.[32] Not even a common destiny is predictable.

The good fortune of the middle class reminds historians of the experience of countless immigrant groups who found Texas a setting for new beginnings. Less sanguine are the prospects for the poorer masses (their numbers continuously augmented by new arrivals from Mexico) who struggle for improvement even though they no longer face the same kinds of barriers that had restrained their forbears.

Glossary

adobes Homes constructed of bricks made from mud mixed with straw.

arrieros Freighters, cart drivers.

barrios Texas-Mexican neighborhoods or enclaves.

Béxar The shortened name for San Antonio (de Béxar), Texas, during the colonial era.

Bexareño A resident of Béxar.

botas Name of a political club in South Texas during the late nineteenth and early twentieth centuries. Literal meaning is *boots*.

braceros Men from Mexico contracted to work in the United States during World War II and through 1964. Literal meaning is *one who works with his arms*.

cabrito A delectable dish made from goat meat (usually that of a kid).

campesino/a A farm worker.

cantina A saloon or barroom.

caudillo In Latin America, a political chieftain, who rules through force.

causa (la) *The cause*. Reference to the cause of Mexican Americans during the Chicano Movement of the 1960s and 1970s.

Chicano An in-group label used among Mexican Americans. Used politically during the 1960s and 1970s.

Cinco de Mayo *May 5*. Reference to a Battle in Puebla, Mexico, on May 5, 1862, in which the native Mexican army repelled a superior French force.

colonia Until about the 1950s, a reference to a Mexican neighborhood (or neighborhoods) in a city. Presently applied to unincorporated, poverty stricken areas of towns in the Texas border region.

compadre The relationship assumed by an individual with the parents of a person whom she/he sponsors at baptism or confirmation. One who stands as the best man at a wedding ceremony also becomes compadre to the parents of the couple receiving the sacrament.

congreso *Congress.*

conjunto A musical ensemble which features the accordion as its lead instrument.

conquistadores Spaniards who reconquered Spain from the Moors or who conquered Latin America for Spain in the sixteenth century.

corridos Folk ballads.

cortito (el) The short-handled hoe used for working in onion, lettuce, and carrot fields.

cuida la honra *Protect your honor, your chastity.*

curanderismo The art of folk healing.

curandero/a One who practices curanderismo; a folk healer.

Diez y Seis de Septiembre *Sixteenth of September.* Reference to the date in 1810 when Father Miguel Hidalgo y Costilla issued the Grito de Dolores calling for Mexico's independence from Spain.

Escuadrón Volante "Flying Squadron" composed of LULACers who visited Texas communities during the 1930s in the effort to organize more councils and spread the LULAC message.

fandango A festive occasion during which the revelers engaged in dancing or social carousing. Also refers to a specific dance.

fiestas patrias The festive commemoration of the Mexican national holidays of Cinco de Mayo and Diez y Seis de Septiembre.

gente (la) *The people*; the Mexican-American community.

gringo/a Spanish for Anglo American.

Grito de Dolores The cry for independence issued by Father Miguel Hidalgo y Costilla on September 16, 1810, in Dolores, Guanajuato.

guaraches Name of a political club in South Texas during the late nineteenth and early twentieth centuries. Literal meaning is *sandals*.

hacienda A rural estate in Mexico worked by peons.

honra *Honor, chastity.*

jacales Makeshift homes built by Tejanos. Usually constructed of mesquite posts, with walls daubed with mud. Thatched coverings served as roofs.

jefe *Chief.* Reference to truckers who transported migrant workers to fields throughout Texas, circa 1920s to 1950s.

ley de fuga   A form of execution applied in the frontier. Assumes that prisoners were killed while trying to escape.

los del otra lado   The people from the other side of the Rio Grande; the people from Mexico.

machismo   A male personality trait emphasizing prowess and virility.

mesteños   Wild herds of livestock in the colonial Texas frontier.

mestizaje   A process of racial congress that took place from the sixteenth through the eighteenth centuries among Spaniards; the indigenous tribes of Latin Americans and Africans.

mestizo   A person who descends from the union of a Spanish male and a female belonging to the Native American tribes.

México de afuera   Reference by people of Mexico to their compatriots living in the United States. Literal meaning is *Mexico of the outside*.

mojados   "Wetbacks." Persons from Mexico who reside in the United States illegally.

movimiento (el)   The Chicano Movement of the 1960s to 1970s.

mutualistas   Mutual aid societies, benefit associations.

noche triste (la)   The night on June 30, 1520, when the Aztecs inflicted devasting casualties on Spanish occupiers of Tenochtitlán as the Iberians sought to escape the Aztec capital.

nopalitos   A delectable dish made from cactus leaves.

obreros   *Laborers*.

pal wes   Going to West Texas to pick farm crops.

partera   A midwife.

pastores   Sheep herders.

patria   The country, or the motherland (Mexico).

patrón   A political boss or a ranch/farm owner.

peones   Members of the peasantry; commoners.

plan   A political platform (or plan) proposed by an opposition group in a movement to overthrow an existing government. If the rebellion succeeds, the new platform will be implemented.

pobladores   Settlers, those who populate.

pocho/a   A term used by people from Mexico to label Mexican Americans who have lost elements of their Mexican culture.

presidio   A Spanish military garrison.

rancho   A ranch.

raza (la)   *The people*. Reference to Mexican Americans as a community.

reconquista   The reconquest of Spain from the Moors, circa eighth to fifteenth centuries.

ricos   The rich, or the wealthier class.

rinches   Spanish for Texas Rangers.

Tejanito/a   A young Mexican American, about school age.

Tejano/a   A person of Spanish-Mexican descent who lives in Texas.

traque   The rail, a reference to the railroad tracks.

troquero   Trucker who transported migrant workers to fields throughout Texas, circa 1920s to 1950s.

vaquero   One who works with cattle. A cowhand.

wes (el)   West Texas.

Notes

PREFACE

[1] Carlos Muñoz, Jr., *Youth, Identity, Power: The Chicano Movement* (New York: Verso, 1989), pp. 64, 70, 71, 78, 134–135, 145.

[2] David J. Weber, "John Francis Bannon and the Historiography of the Spanish Borderlands: Retrospect and Prospect," in Weber (ed.), *Myth and the History of the Hispanic Southwest* (Albuquerque: University of New Mexico Press, 1988), pp. 69–71.

[3] Gerald E. Poyo and Gilberto M. Hinojosa, *Tejano Origins in Eighteenth-Century San Antonio* (Austin: University of Texas Press, 1991), pp. xiv-xix; Arnoldo De León, "Texas-Mexicans: Twentieth Century Interpretations," in Walter L. Buenger and Robert A. Calvert (eds.), *Texas Through Time: Evolving Interpretations* (College Station: Texas A&M University Press, 1991), pp. 20–49.

CHAPTER ONE

[1] Gilbert R. Cruz, *Let There be Towns: Spanish Municipal Origins in the American Southwest, 1610–1810* (College Station: Texas A&M University Press, 1988), pp. 5–6.

[2] Robert Ryal Miller, *Mexico: A History* (Norman: University of Oklahoma Press, 1985), Chapter 3.

[3] John Francis Bannon, et al., *Latin America* (4th ed.; Encino, Calif: Glencoe Press, 1977), p. 89.

[4] Ibid., pp. 90–91.

[5] Carlos Eduardo Castañeda, *The Mission Era: The Winning of Texas, 1693–1751*, vol. II of *Our Catholic Heritage in Texas, 1519–1936* (7 vols; Austin: Von Boeckmann-Jones Co., 1936–1958; reprinted by New York: Arno Press, 1976), pp. 46 (n22), pp. 47, 59–60.

[6] Cruz, *Let There Be Towns*, p. 90; Jack Jackson, *Los Mesteños: Spanish Ranching in Texas* (College Station: Texas A&M University Press, 1986), pp. 13–14.

[7] Cruz, *Let There Be Towns*, pp. 82, 86–87.

[8] Oakah, L. Jones, *Los Paisanos: Spanish Settlers on the Northern Frontier of New Spain* (Norman: University of Oklahoma Press, 1979), p. 47.

[9] Cruz, *Let There Be Towns* pp. 94–95, 128–129; Jones, *Los Paisanos*, p. 70.

[10] Jesús F. de la Teja, "Forgotten Founders: The Military Settlers of Eighteenth-Century San Antonio de Béxar," in Gerald E. Poyo and Gilberto M. Hinojosa, *Tejano Origins in Eighteenth-Century San Antonio* (Austin: University of Texas Press, 1991), pp. 29–30, 38; and Gerald E. Poyo, "Immigrants and Integration in Late Eighteenth-Century Béxar," in ibid., p. 85.

[11] Juan Gómez Quiñones, *Making of the*

Mexican Working Class North of the Rio Bravo (Los Angeles: Aztlán Publications, 1977), pp. 5–6; Poyo, "Immigrants and Integration in Late Eighteenth-Century Béxar," p. 86; Cruz, *Let There Be Towns*, p. 127.

[12] Gerald E. Poyo and Gilberto M. Hinojosa, "Spanish Texas and Borderlands Historiography in Transition: Implications for United States History," *Journal of American History*, 75 (September, 1988), 408, 409, 410; John R. Chávez, *The Lost Land: The Chicano Image of the Southwest* (Albuquerque: University of New Mexico Press, 1984), p. 31.

[13] Gómez-Quiñones, *Making of the Mexican Working Class*, p. 7.

[14] Herbert E. Bolton, "The Mission As A Frontier Institution in the Spanish American Colonies," in David J. Weber (ed.), *New Spain's Far Northern Frontier: Essays on Spain in the American West, 1540–1821* (Albuquerque: University of New Mexico Press, 1979), pp. 49–65; Gilberto M. Hinojosa, "The Enduring Hispanic Faith Communities: Spanish and Texas Church Historiography," *The Journal of Texas Catholic History and Culture*, I (March, 1990), 22, 27–28.

[15] Max L. Moorhead, *The Presidio: Bastion of the Spanish Borderlands* (Norman: University of Oklahoma Press, 1975), pp. 3–4; Gilberto M. Hinojosa, "The Religious-Indian Communities: The Goals of the Friars," in Poyo and Hinojosa, *Tejano Origins in Eighteenth-Century San Antonio*, p. 79.

[16] de la Teja, "Forgotten Founders," pp. 30, 33; Jesús F. de la Teja, "Land and Society in 18th Century San Antonio de Béxar: A Community in New Spain's Northern Frontier" (Ph.D. Dissertation, University of Texas, 1988), pp. 385–386, 255, 273–276.

[17] de la Teja, "Land and Society," pp. 255, 273–276.

[18] Jackson, *Los Mesteños*, pp. 11, 12–13, 30; Sandra L. Myers, *The Ranch in Spanish Texas, 1691–1800* (El Paso: Texas Western Press, 1969), pp. 12–13.

[19] Jackson, *Los Mesteños*, p. 52.

[20] de la Teja, "Land and Society," p. 267; Myers, *Ranching in Spanish Texas*, pp. 16, 15.

[21] Poyo and Hinojosa, "Spanish Texas and Borderlands Historiography in Transition," p. 406.

[22] Ibid., p. 407; Jackson, *Los Mesteños*, pp. 130, 131; de la Teja, "Land and Society," pp. 255, 256.

[23] Poyo and Hinojosa, "Spanish Texas and Borderlands Historiography," p. 408.

[24] Jones, *Los Paisanos*, pp. 54; Poyo and Hinojosa, *Tejano Origins in Eighteenth Century San Antonio*, p. 138.

[25] Poyo, "Immigrants and Integration in Eighteenth-Century Béxar," pp. 90–96; Cruz, *Let There Be Towns*, p. 128.

[26] James Michael McReynolds, "Family Life in a Borderlands Community: Nacogdoches, Texas, 1779–1861," (Ph.D. Dissertation, Texas Tech University, 1978), Chapter II.

[27] Jones, *Los Paisanos*, pp. 60–61.

[28] Jesús F. de la Teja, "Indians, Soldiers, and Canary Islanders: The Making of a Texas Frontier Community," *Locus*, III (Fall, 1990), 82, 85, 89; Also see, Poyo and Hinojosa, *Tejano Origins in Eighteenth Century San Antonio*, pp. xx-xxi, 137.

[29] Cruz, *Let There Be Towns*, p. 170.

[30] de la Teja, "Land and Society," p. 368.

[31] Jackson, *Los Mesteños*, p. 130.

[32] Poyo and Hinojosa, *Tejano Origins in Eighteenth Century San Antonio*, p. 140.

[33] Odie B. Faulk, *A Successful Failure* (Austin: Steck-Vaughn, 1965), pp. 176–178; Odie B. Faulk, *The Last Years of Spanish Texas* (London: The Hague Paris Press, 1964), pp. 50, 109–112.

[34] de la Teja, "Indians, Soldiers, and Canary Islanders," pp. 88, 95.

[35] Ibid., p. 95; Gómez-Quiñones, *Making of Mexican Working Class*, p. 12.

[36] Jones, *Los Paisanos*, p. 60; Poyo, "Immigrants and Integration in Eighteenth-Century Béxar," pp. 85–86; Cruz, *Let There Be Towns*, p. 129.

[37] de la Teja, "Land and Society," pp. 93–103; Gerald E. Poyo, "The Canary Islands Immigrants of San Antonio: From Ethnic Exclusivity to Community in Eighteenth-

Century Béxar," in Poyo and Hinojosa, *Tejano Origins in Eighteenth Century San Antonio*, p. 47; de la Teja, "Forgotten Founders," in ibid., pp. 32–33; Poyo, "Immigrants and Integration in Late Eighteenth Century Béxar," in ibid., pp. 96–97; and Gilberto M. Hinojosa and Anne E. Fox, "Indians and Their Culture in San Fernando de Béxar," in ibid., pp. 106–107; and Alicia V. Tjarks, "Comparative Demographic Analysis of Texas, 1777–1793," *Southwestern Historical Quarterly*, LXXVII (January, 1974), 322–338.

38 Tjarks, "Comparative Demographic Analysis," p. 294; de la Teja, "Land and Society," pp. 92–93, 102, 103, 113–114; Poyo, "Immigrants and Integration in Late Eighteenth-Century Béxar," pp. 86–87.

39 David J. Weber, *The Mexican Frontier, 1821–1848: The American Southwest Under Mexico* (Albuquerque: University of New Mexico Press, 1982), pp. 215–216.

40 Colin M. MacLachlan and Jaime E. Rodríguez-O, *The Forging of the Cosmic Race: A Reinterpretation of Colonial Mexico* (Berkeley: University of California Press, 1980), pp. 296–297.

41 Jackson, *Los Mesteños*, pp. 294–295.

42 Poyo and Hinojosa, "Spanish Texas and Borderlands Historiography," p. 414; de la Teja, "Land and Society," pp. 270–271.

43 Poyo and Hinojosa, "Spanish Texas and Borderlands Historiography," pp. 415, 412.

44 Poyo, "The Canary Islands Immigrants of San Antonio," pp. 57–58.

CHAPTER TWO

1 Seymour V. Connor, *Texas: A History* (Arlington Heights: Harlan Davidson, Inc., 1971), p. 57; Gilberto M. Hinojosa, *A Borderlands Town in Transition* (College Station: Texas A&M Press, 1983), p. 32.

2 David J. Weber, *The Mexican Frontier, 1821–1848: The American Southwest Under Mexico* (Albuquerque: University of New Mexico Press, 1982), p. 280.

3 Ibid., p. 284; Miguel León-Portilla, "The Norteño Variety of Mexican Culture: An Ethnohistorical Approach," in Edward H. Spicer and Raymond H. Thompson (eds.), *Plural Society in the Southwest* (Albuquer-

que: University of New Mexico Press, 1972), pp. 109–114.

4 Gerald E. Poyo and Gilberto M. Hinojosa, *Tejano Origins in Eighteenth-Century San Antonio* (Austin: University of Texas Press, 1991), pp. 140, 141.

5 Gerald E. Poyo and Gilberto M. Hinojosa, "Spanish Texas and Borderlands Historiography in Transition: Implications for United States History," *Journal of American History*, 75 (September, 1988), 411–412, 413; Jesús F. de la Teja, "Rebellion in the Frontier" (unpublished paper in author's files).

6 Weber, *The Mexican Frontier*, pp. 9–10; Jack Jackson, *Los Mesteños: Spanish Ranching in Texas* (College Station: Texas A&M University Press, 1986), p. 526; Félix D. Almaráz, Jr., *Tragic Cavalier: Manuel Salcedo of Texas* (Austin: University of Texas Press, 1970), p. 119. de la Teja, "Rebellion in the Frontier," is a revisionist work on this episode of Texas history (unpublished paper in author's files).

7 Jackson, *Los Mesteños*, p. 527.

8 Weber, *The Mexican Frontier*, p. 9.

9 Jackson, *Los Mesteños*, pp. 528, 530–533.

10 Almaráz, *Tragic Cavalier*, pp. 188–124; Weber, *The Mexican Frontier*, p. 10.

11 Jackson, *Los Mesteños*, pp. 537, 555.

12 Ibid., pp. 526, 546–547.

13 Weber, *The Mexican Frontier*, p. 10.

14 Carey McWilliams, *North From Mexico: The Spanish Speaking People of the United States* (New York: Greenwood Press, 1968), pp. 153, 154, 155, 156, 146.

15 Donald E. Worcester, "The Significance of the Spanish Borderlands in the United States," in David J. Weber (ed.), *New Spain's Far Northern Frontier: Essays on Spain in the American West, 1540–1821* (Albuquerque: University of New Mexico Press, 1979), pp. 4–10; Pauline Kibbe, *Latin Americans in Texas* (Albuquerque: University of New Mexico Press, 1946), p. 34; McWilliams, *North From Mexico*, pp. 153–154; Paul H. Carlson, *Texas Woolybacks: The Texas Sheep and Goat Industry* (College Station: Texas A&M University Press, 1982), p. 17.

16 Weber, *The Mexican Frontier*, p. 160.

[17] Juan N. Almonte, "Statistical Report on Texas," translated by C. E. Castañeda, *Southwestern Historical Quarerly*, XXVIII (January 1925), 186, 206. Also see, *The Handbook of Victoria County* (Austin: The Texas State Historical Association, 1990), p. 113, and Hinojosa, *A Borderland Town in Transition*, p. 45.

[18] Jesús F. de la Teja and John Wheat, "Béxar: Profile of a Tejano Community, 1820–1832," *Southwestern Historical Quarterly*, 89 (July, 1985), 28.

[19] de la Teja and Wheat, "Béxar," pp. 19–20; Félix D. Almaráz, Jr., "The Warp and the Weft: An Overview of the Social Fabric of Mexican Texas," *East Texas Historical Journal*, 27, No. 2 (1989), 18.

[20] Gilberto M. Hinojosa, "The Enduring Hispanic Faith Communities: Spanish and Texas Church Historiography," *The Journal of Texas Catholic History and Culture*, I (March, 1990), 30–31, 35.

[21] Jackson, *Los Mesteños*, pp. 596–597; de la Teja and Wheat, "Béxar," pp. 26, 28.

[22] de la Teja and Wheat, "Béxar," pp. 26, 28.

[23] Jackson, *Los Mesteños*, p. 592; Paul S. Taylor, *An American Mexican Frontier: Nueces County, Texas* (Chapel Hill: University of North Carolina Press, 1934), pp. 10–13; Hinojosa, *A Borderland Town in Transition*, p. 42.

[24] de la Teja and Wheat, "Béxar," p. 26; Weber, *The Mexican Frontier*, pp. 140–141.

[25] Andreas V. Reichstein, *Rise of The Lone Star: The Making of Texas* (College Station: Texas A&M University Press, 1989), pp. 87–88; Weber, *The Mexican Frontier*, p. 208.

[26] Reichstein, *Rise of the Lone Star*, pp. 87–88; de la Teja and Wheat, "Béxar," pp. 10, 23.

[27] Weber, *The Mexican Frontier*, pp. 215–216; Richard Griswold del Castillo, *La Familia: Chicano Families in the Urban Southwest, 1840 to the Present* (Notre Dame: University of Notre Dame Press, 1984), pp. 30, 28–29.

[28] Fane Downs, "'Tryels and Trubbles': Women in Early Nineteenth Century Texas," *Southwestern Historical Quarterly*, 90 (July, 1986), 45, 55–56.

[29] Weber, *The Mexican Frontier*, pp. 158–161, 164.

[30] de la Teja and Wheat, "Béxar," pp. 30–31; Jesús F. de la Teja, *A Revolution Remembered: The Memoirs and Selected Correspondence Of Juan N. Seguin* (Austin: State House Press, 1991), pp. 7, 10, 15; David J. Weber, *Myth and the History of the Hispanic Southwest* (Albuquerque: University of New Mexico Press, 1988), pp. 145–146.

[31] Reichstein, *Rise of the Lone Star*, p. 55; Weber, *Myth and the History of the Hispanic Southwest*, pp. 147–148; and Almonte, "Statistical Report on Texas," p. 207.

[32] Randolph B. Campbell, *An Empire For Slavery: The Peculiar Institution in Texas, 1821–1865* (Baton Rouge: Louisiana State University Press, 1989), pp. 25–27.

[33] Weber, *The Mexican Frontier*, p. 177.

[34] Weber, *Myth and the History of the Hispanic Southwest*, p. 144; Jackson, *Los Mesteños*, p. 599; Alwyn Barr, *Texans in Revolt: The Battle for San Antonio, 1835* (Austin: University of Texas Press, 1990), p. 12.

[35] Rodolfo F. Acuña, *Occupied America* (3rd ed.; New York: Harper and Row, 1988), p. 10.; Rodolfo F. Acuña, "Inside the Alamo: A Dispatch From Bexar County," *Texas Observer*, January 26, 1990, p. 23; Tom Glaser, "Victory or Death," in Susan P. Schoelwer, *Alamo Images: Changing Perceptions of a Texas Experience* (Dallas: DeGolyer Library and SMU Press, 1985), p. 76.

[36] Richard Santos, *Santa Anna's Campaign Against Texas* (Waco: Texian Press, 1970), pp. 17, 34, 63; Glaser, "Victory or Death," pp. 85–86.

[37] Santos, *Santa Anna's Campaign Against Texas*, pp. 74–76; Glaser, "Victory or Death," pp. 83, 85, 92, 94.

[38] Thomas Lloyd Miller, "Mexican Texans at the Alamo," *Journal of Mexican American History*, II (Fall, 1971), 33.

[39] David J. Weber, *Foreigners in Their Native Land: Historical Roots of the Mexican Americans* (Albuquerque: University of New Mexico Press), p. 92.

[40] H. M. Henderson, "A Critical Analysis of the San Jacinto Campaign," *Southwestern*

Historical Quarterly, 59 (January, 1956), 344–362; Eugene C. Barker, "The San Jacinto Campaign," *Quarterly of the Texas State Historical Association*, IV (July, 1900), 271, 291.

[41] Weber, *The Mexican Frontier*, p. 251.

[42] Paul D. Lack, *The Texas Revolutionary Experience: A Social and Politial History* (College Station: Texas A&M University Press, 1992), pp. 183–207; Weber, *Foreigners in Their Native Land*, p. 93.

[43] Fernando V. Padilla, "Early Chicano Legal Recognition, 1846–1897," *Journal of Popular Culture*, XIII (Spring, 1980), 564–565.

CHAPTER THREE

[1] Oscar J. Martínez, "On the Size of the Chicano Population: New Estimates, 1850–1900," *Aztlán: International Journal of Chicano Studies Research*, VI (Spring, 1975), 54; Emilio Zamora, Jr., "Mexican Labor Activity in South Texas, 1900–1920" (Ph.D. Dissertation, University of Texas, 1983), pp. 28–29; Arnoldo De León and Kenneth L. Stewart, *Tejanos and the Numbers Game: A Socio-Historical Interpretation from the Federal Censuses, 1850–1900* (Albuquerque: University of New Mexico Press, 1989), p. 24.

[2] Neil Foley, "Mexican Migrant and Tenant Labor in Central Texas Cotton Counties, 1880–1930," *Wooster Review*, No. 9 (Spring, 1989), 90–91; Arnoldo De León, *The Tejano Community, 1836–1900* (Albuquerque: University of New Mexico Press, 1982), pp. 63–65; Arnoldo De León and Kenneth L. Stewart, "Tejano Demographic Patterns and Socio-economic Development," *The Borderlands Journal*, VII (Fall, 1983), 3–4.

[3] De León and Stewart, "Tejano Demographic Patterns," p. 2.

[4] W. H. Timmons, "The El Paso Area in the Mexican Period," *Southwestern Historical Quarterly*, 84 (July, 1980), 26–28; C. L. Sonnichsen, *Pass of the North* (El Paso: Texas Western Press, 1968), p. 442, n2; De León and Stewart, "Tejano Demographic Patterns," pp. 1–3.

[5] Paul D. Lack, *The Texas Revolutionary Experience: A Social and Political History* (College Station: Texas A&M University Press,

1992), pp. 183–207; Arnoldo De León, *They Called Them Greasers: Anglo Attitudes Toward Mexicans in Texas* (Austin: University of Texas Press, 1983), p. 77.

[6] De León, *They Called Them Greasers*, p. 78.

[7] De León, *The Tejano Community*, pp. 15–16; Ellen Schneider and Paul H. Carlson, "Gunnysackers, *Carreteros*, and Teamsters: The South Texas Cart War of 1857," *The Journal of South Texas*, I (Spring, 1988), pp. 1–9.

[8] De León, *The Tejano Community*, pp. 17–18; Jerry Don Thompson, "The Many Faces of Juan Nepomuceno Cortina," in *South Texas Studies*, II (Victoria, Tex.: Victoria College Press, 1991), pp. 85–98; "Juan N. Cortina," in Pedro Castillo and Albert Camarillo (eds.), *Furia y Muerte: Los Bandidos Chicanos* (Los Angeles: Aztlán Publications, 1973), pp. 84–112; Rodolfo Acuña, *Occupied America: A History of Chicanos* (3rd. ed.; New York: Harper and Row, 1988), pp. 44–46.

[9] De León, *The Tejano Community*, pp. 19–20.

[10] Ibid., pp. 20–21; *Handbook of Texas*, II (2 vols; Austin: Texas State Historical Association, 1952), pp. 536–537.

[11] Jack Jackson, *Los Mesteños: Spanish Ranching in Texas, 1721–1821* (College Station: A&M University Press, 1986), pp. 613–615.

[12] David Montejano, *Anglos and Mexicans in the Making of Texas* (Austin: University of Texas Press, 1987), pp. 34–37; Jane Dysart, "Mexican Women in San Antonio, 1830–1860: The Assimilation Process," *Western Historical Quarterly*, VII (October, 1976), 370, 371.

[13] Walter Prescott Webb, *The Texas Rangers: A Century of Frontier Defense* (New York: Houghton Mifflin Co., 1935), p. 175; De León, *The Tejano Community*, p. 46.

[14] Montejano, *Anglos and Mexicans in the Making of Texas*, p. 40.

[15] Ibid., pp. 37–38, 41.

[16] De León, *They Called Them Greasers*, p. 88.

[17] Jackson, *Los Mesteños*, pp. 615–616.

[18] Montejano, *Anglos and Mexicans in the*

Making of Texas, pp. 50–51, 56–58, 59, 60, 63, 68–70.

[19] De León, *The Tejano Community*, pp. 67–68.

[20] Jackson, *Los Mesteños*, p. 610.

[21] De León, *The Tejano Community*, pp. 50, 52, 57–58.

[22] Montejano, *Anglos and Mexicans in the Making of Texas*, pp. 79–84.

[23] De León and Stewart, *Tejanos and the Numbers Game*, p. 68.

[24] Ibid., p. 92.

[25] De León, *The Tejano Community*, p. 104.

[26] Ibid., pp. 114–118, 172–177, 195–201 passim.

[27] Ibid., pp. 158, 176–177, 204–206; Guadalupe San Miguel, Jr., *"Let All of Them Take Heed": Mexican Americans and the Campaign for Educational Equality in Texas, 1910–1981* (Austin: University of Texas Press, 1987), p. 9.

[28] Montejano, *Anglos and Mexicans in the Making of Texas*, pp. 34, 51; Dysart, "Mexican Women in San Antonio," pp. 370–371.

[29] De León, *The Tejano Community*, pp. 79–81.

[30] Montejano, *Anglos and Mexicans in the Making of Texas*, p. 47.

[31] De León, *The Tejano Community*, pp. 96–97, 98–100.

[32] Ibid., pp. 174, 185, 118, 134.

[33] Kenneth L. Stewart and Arnoldo De León, *Not Room Enough: Mexicans, Anglos, and Socio-Economic Change in Texas, 1850–1900* (Albuquerque: University of New Mexico Press, forthcoming).

[34] Jesús F. de la Teja (ed.), *A Revolution Remembered: The Memoirs and Selected Correspondence of Juan N. Seguín* (Austin: State House Press, 1991), pp. 40–50.

[35] Walter L. Buenger, *Secession and the Union in Texas* (Austin: University of Texas Press, 1984), pp. 90, 91, 94, 95.

[36] Jerry Don Thompson, *Mexican Texans in the Union Army* (El Paso: Texas Western Press, 1986), pp. vii–ix; Jerry Don Thompson, *Vaqueros in Blue and Gray* (Austin: Presidial Press, 1976), pp. 5, 25, 81.

[37] See for example, Jerry Don Thompson, *Warm Weather and Bad Whiskey: The 1886 Laredo Election Riot* (El Paso: Texas West-

ern Press, 1991); Carlysle Graham Raht, *Romance of Davis Mountains and Big Bend Country* (El Paso: The Raht Books Co., 1919), p. 216; Arnoldo De León, *San Angeleños* (San Angelo: Fort Concho Museum Press, 1985).

[38] James Ernest Crisp, "Anglo-Texan Attitudes Toward the Mexicans, 1821–1845" (Ph.D. Dissertation, Yale Univeristy, 1976), pp. 399–403, 408–450; Buenger, *Secession and the Union in Texas*, pp. 85, 90–91, 95, 104; Joseph Martin Dawson, *Jose Antonio Navarro: Co-Creator of Texas* (Waco: Baylor University Press, 1969); Stewart and De León, *Not Room Enough*, forthcoming.

[39] John Denny Riley, "Santos Benavides: His Influence on the Lower Rio Grande, 1823–1891" (Ph.D. Dissertation, Texas Christian University, 1976), pp. 256–257, 263–264; Stewart and De León, *Not Room Enough*, forthcoming.

[40] Buenger, *Secession and the Union in Texas*, pp. 90–91; Stewart and De León, *Not Room Enough*, forthcoming; Thompson, "The Many Faces of Juan Nepomuceno Cortina," pp. 92–93.

CHAPTER FOUR

[1] Arnoldo De León, *They Called Them Greasers: Anglo Attitudes Toward Mexicans in Texas, 1821–1900* (Austin: University of Texas Press, 1983), pp. 93–94, 104–105; José E. Limón, "Healing the Wounds: Folk Symbols and Historical Crisis," *The Texas Humanist*, VI (March-April, 1984), pp. 22–23.

[2] Arnoldo De León, *The Tejano Community, 1836–1900* (Albuquerque: University of New Mexico Press, 1982), p. 25.

[3] David Montejano, *Anglos and Mexicans in the Making of Texas, 1836–1986* (Austin: University of Texas Press, 1987), p. 110.

[4] Ibid., pp. 104, 91, 109.

[5] Robert A. Calvert and Arnoldo De León, *The History of Texas* (Arlington Heights: Harlan Davidson, Inc., 1990), pp. 169, 182, 186, 189, 215–216.

[6] Mario T. García, *Desert Immigrants: The Mexicans of El Paso, 1880–1920* (New Haven: Yale University Press, 1981), pp. 9–32.

[7] Montejano, *Anglos and Mexicans in the*

Making of Texas, pp. 94, 95, 107; Calvert and De León, *The History of Texas*, p. 170.
[8] Montejano, *Anglos and Mexicans in the Making of Texas*, p. 130; Calvert and De León, *The History of Texas*, p. 252.
[9] Emilio Zamora, Jr., "Mexican Labor Activity in South Texas, 1900–1920" (Ph.D. Dissertation, University of Texas at Austin, 1983), pp. 28–29.
[10] Arnoldo De León and Kenneth L. Stewart, "Tejano Demographic Patterns and Socio-Economic Development," *The Borderlands Journal*, VII (Fall, 1983), 6.
[11] Neil Foley, "Mexican Migrant and Tenant Labor in in Central Texas Cotton Counties, 1880–1930," *Wooster Review*, No. 9 (Spring, 1989), 91.
[12] Stuart Jamieson, *Labor Unionism in American Agriculture* (New York: Arno Press, 1976), p. 260.
[13] Arnoldo De León and Kenneth L. Stewart, *Tejanos and the Numbers Game: A Sociohistorical Profile from the Federal Censuses, 1850–1900* (Albuqurque: University of New Mexico Press, 1989), pp. 33 (Table 3.2), 37–38.
[14] De León, *The Tejano Community*, pp. 97, 96.
[15] Montejano, *Anglos and Mexicans in the Making of Texas*, p. 72.
[16] De Leon, *The Tejano Community*, pp. 80, 81–82, 84.
[17] Ibid., pp. 35–42; Montejano, *Anglos and Mexicans in the Making of Texas*, pp. 95, 129.
[18] De León, *The Tejano Community*, pp. 42–44.
[19] Ibid., pp. 33–34.
[20] Ibid., pp. 46–47.
[21] Evan Anders, *Boss Rule in South Texas: The Progressive Era* (Austin: University of Texas Press, 1982), p. 89.
[22] Ibid., Chapter 3.
[23] Zamora, "Mexican Labor Activity," pp. 81–82.
[24] Ibid., p. 81.
[25] Mario T. García, "Racial Dualism in the El Paso Labor Market, 1880–1920," *Aztlán: International Journal of Chicano Studies Research*, VI (Summer, 1975), 213.
[26] Zamora, "Mexican Labor Activity," p. 82; Rodolfo F. Acuña, *Occupied America:*

A History of Chicanos (3rd ed.; New York: Harper and Row, 1988), p. 156.
[27] Zamora, "Mexican Labor Activity," pp. 149, 151, 116–117, 142, 146, 147.
[28] Lawrence A. Cardoso, *Mexican Emigration to the United States, 1897–1931* (Tucson: University of Arizona Press, 1980), pp. 27–29.
[29] Zamora, "Mexican Labor Activity," p. 29; De León and Stewart, *Tejanos and Numbers Game*, pp. 28–29; Terry G. Jordan, "A Century and a Half of Ethnic Change in Texas, 1836–1986," *Southwestern Historical Quarterly*, 89 (April, 1982), 394.
[30] De León and Stewart, *Tejanos and Numbers Game*, pp. 85, 86–88.
[31] Jovita González, "America Invades the Border Towns," *Southwest Review*, XV (Summer, 1930), 469.
[32] De León and Stewart, *Tejanos and Numbers Game*, pp. 67–68.
[33] Montejano, *Anglos and Mexicans in the Making of Texas*, p. 91; David Montejano, *Race, Labor Repression, and Capitalist Agriculture: Notes from South Texas, 1920–1930* (Berkeley: Institute for the Study of Social Change, 1977), p. 7.
[34] Paul H. Carlson, *Texas Woolybacks: The Texas Sheep and Goat Industry* (College Station: Texas A&M University Press, 1982), pp. 86, 87, 88–92, 95, 97, 99, 100.
[35] De León and Stewart, *Tejanos and Numbers Game*, pp. 33, 34–35.
[36] Guadalupe San Miguel, Jr., "Social and Educational Influences Shaping the Mexican American Mind," *Journal of Midwest History of Education Society*, XIV (1986), 62; González, "America Invades the Border Towns," p. 474.
[37] Ben Procter and Archie P. McDonald, *The Texas Heritage* (Arlington Heights: Forum Press, 1980), p. 173.
[38] De León and Stewart, *Tejanos and Numbers Game*, pp. 45–46.
[39] Ibid., p. 45.
[40] Zamora, "Mexican Labor Activity," pp. 98–100; Juan Goméz-Quiñones, *Sembradores: Ricardo Flores Magón and the Partido Liberal Mexicano* (Los Angeles: Chicano Studies Research Center, 1976), pp. 29, 35–36.

[41] De León, *The Tejano Community*, pp. 150–151.

[42] Limón, "Healing the Wounds," pp. 22–23.

[43] Américo Paredes, "José Mosqueda and the Folklorization of Actual Events," *Aztlán: Chicano Journal of the Social Sciences and the Arts*, IV (Spring, 1973), 5–6, 14.

[44] Rodolfo Rocha, "The Sting and Power of Rebellion," *The Texas Humanist*, VI (March-April, 1984), 20; Américo Paredes, *A Texas-Mexican Cancionero* (Urbana: University of Illinois Press, 1976), p. 32.

[45] Limón, "Healing the Wounds," pp. 22–23.

[46] Gilbert M. Cuthbertson, "Catarino Garza and the Garza War," *Texana*, XII (No. 4), 337.

[47] De León, *They Called Them Greasers*, pp. 60–61.

[48] Cuthbertson, "Catarino Garza," p. 345.

CHAPTER FIVE

[1] Carey McWilliams, *North From Mexico* (New York: Greenwood Press, 1968), p. 163; Ricardo Romo, "The Urbanization of Southwestern Chicanos," in Ricardo Romo and Raymund Paredes, *New Directions in Chicano Scholarship* (La Jolla: University of California at San Diego, 1978), p. 194.

[2] Mario T. García, "La Frontera: The Border as Symbol and Reality," *Estudios Mexicanos/Mexican Studies*, I (Summer, 1985), 197.

[3] Lawrence Cardoso, *Mexican Emigration to the United States* (Tucson: University of Arizona Press, 1980), pp. 2, 6–7, 9–10.

[4] Arthur Corwin, *Immigrants—and Immigrants* (Westport, Ct: Greenwood Press, 1978), pp. 46, 52.

[5] Quoted in Mark Reisler, *By the Sweat of Their Brow* (Westport, Ct: Greenwood Press, 1976), p. 40.

[6] Cardoso, *Mexican Emigration to the United States*, pp. 28–29, 46.

[7] Ibid., pp. 83, 129–130; Wayne A. Cornelius, "Mexican Immigration to the United States: Causes, Consequences, and United States Responses" (Cambridge: MIT, 1978), pp. 3, 7.

[8] R. Reynolds McKay, "Texas Mexican Repatriation During the Great Depression" (Ph.D. Dissertation, University of Oklahoma at Norman, 1982), p. 66.

[9] David Montejano, *Anglos and Mexicans in the Making of Texas, 1836–1986* (Austin: University of Texas Press, 1987), pp. 180, 186–188.

[10] Ibid., pp. 183, 188.

[11] Ibid., pp. 183, 189, 179, 190.

[12] Ibid., pp. 182, 190; Corwin, *Immigrants—and Immigrants*, p.146.

[13] Corwin, *Immigrants—and Immigrants*, p. 45.

[14] Hubert J. Miller, "Mexican Migration to the United States, 1900–1920," *The Borderlands Journal*, VII (Spring, 1984), 180; Corwin, *Immigrants—and Immigrants*, p. 47.

[15] Mario T. García, *Desert Immigrants: The Mexicans of El Paso, 1880–1920* (New Haven: Yale University Press, 1981), p. 2; George Coalson, *The Development of Migrant Farm Labor System in Texas, 1900–1954* (San Francisco: R&E Research Associates, 1977), p. 2; Romo, "Urbanization of Southwestern Chicanos," p. 185.

[16] Arnoldo De León, *San Angeleños: Mexican Americans in San Angelo, Texas* (San Angelo: Fort Concho Museum Press, 1985), p. 35.

[17] Richard A. García, *Rise of the Mexican American Middle Class, San Antonio, 1929–1941* (College Station: Texas A&M University Press, 1991), pp. 28–29.

[18] Neil Foley, "Mexican Migrant and Tenant Labor in Central Texas Cotton Counties, 1880–1930: Social and Economic Transformation in a Multicultural Society," *Wooster Review*, No. 9 (Spring, 1989), 99; McWilliams, *North From Mexico*, p. 170; McKay, "Texas Mexican Repatriation," p. 84.

[19] Arnoldo De León, *Ethnicity in the Sunbelt: A History of Mexican Americans in Houston* (Houston: Mexican American Studies Program, 1989), pp. xv, 7, 23, 10; "A Report on Illiteracy in Texas" (Austin: U. T. Bulletin No. 2328, 1923), p. 12.

[20] *Dallas Morning News*, September 13, 1987, p. 22A, June 29, 1988, p. 2C; Romo, "The Urbanization of Southwestern Chicanos," p. 185; Flora Lowrey,

"Night School in Little Mexico," *Southwest Review*, XVI (October, 1930), 37.

[21] Reisler, *Sweat of Their Brow*, p. 51; Romo, "Urbanization of Southwestern Chicanos," p. 185.

[22] Terry G. Jordan, "A Century and a Half of Ethnic Change in Texas, 1836–1986," *Southwestern Historical Quarterly*, 89 (April, 1986), 399; "A Report on Illiteracy in Texas," p. 11.

[23] Miller, "Mexican Migration to the U.S.," p. 180; García, *Rise of the Mexican American Middle Class*, p. 35.

[24] García, *Rise of the Mexican American Middle Class*, pp. 240–241, 234, 103, 104; Richard A. García, "The Mexican American Mind: A Product of the 1930s," in Mario T. García, *History, Culture, and Society* (Ypsilanti: Bilingual Press/Editorial Bilingue, 1983), pp. 78, 76.

[25] Emory Bogardus, "The Mexican Immigrant and Segregation," *American Journal of Sociology*, XXXVI (July, 1930), 76–77.

[26] Lyle Saunders, *Wetbacks in the Lower Rio Grande Valley* (New York: Arno Press, 1976), p. 61.

[27] Mario T. García, *Mexican Americans: Leadership and Ideology*, 1930–1960 (New Haven: Yale University Press, 1989), pp. 14–15.

[28] García, *Rise of the Mexican American Middle Class*, p. 44, 77, 81–83.

[29] García, *Desert Immigrants*, pp. 74, 75, 76; Mario T. García, "The Chicana in American History: Mexican Women in El Paso," *Pacific Historical Review*, XLIX (May, 1980), 321.

[30] Julie Leininger Pycior, "La Raza Organizes: Mexican American Life in San Antonio, 1915–1930, as Reflected in Mutualista Activities" (Ph.D. Dissertation, University of Notre Dame, 1979), pp. 189, 198.

[31] Yolanda G. Romero, "From Rebels to Immigrants to Chicanas: Hispanic Women in Lubbock County" (M.A. Thesis, Texas Tech Press, 1987), pp. 8, 9, 10.

[32] De León, *Ethnicity in the Sunbelt*, pp. 37, 33–34, 38; Lowrey, "Night School in Little Mexico," p. 39.

[33] Nick Kanellos, "Two Centuries of Hispanic Theatre in the Southwest," *Revista*

Chicano-Riqueña, XI (Spring, 1983), 24–25, 35; Nick Kanellos, *A History of Hispanic Theatre in the United States* (Austin: University of Texas Press, 1990), pp. 180–181, 198, 199–200; Manuel Peña, *The Texas Mexican Conjunto: History of a Working Class Music* (Austin: University of Texas Press, 1985), pp. 29, 35–36, 38.

[34] Manuel Gamio, *Mexican Immigration to the United States* (New York: Arno Press, 1969), p. 129.

[35] De León, *Ethnicity in the Sunbelt*, pp. 31, 75; Pycior, "La Raza Organizes," pp. 94–95.

[36] De León, *Ethnicity in the Sunbelt*, p. 14.

[37] Zamora, "Mexican Labor Activity," pp. 76–77; Juan Gómez Quiñones, *Sembradores: Ricardo Flores Magón and the Partido Liberal Mexicano* (Los Angeles: Chicano Studies Research Center, 1976), p. 29.

[38] Gómez-Quiñones, *Sembradores*, pp. 29, 35–36.

[39] Zamora, "Mexican Labor Activity," pp. 77–78.

[40] García, *Mexican Americans*, p. 175.

[41] Marta Cotera, *Diosa y Hembra* (Austin: Information Systems Development, 1976), pp. 65–66; Gómez-Quiñones, *Sembradores*, p. 36; Rodolfo F. Acuña, *Occupied America: A History of Chicanos* (3rd ed.; New York: Harper and Row, 1988), p. 151.

[42] Zamora, "Mexican Labor Activity," pp. 90–91.

[43] Lowrey, "Night School in Little Mexico," pp. 39–40; John Ernest Gregg, "The History of Presidio County" (Master of Arts Thesis, University of Texas, 1933), pp. 201–202; De León, *Ethnicity in the Sunbelt*, p. 33.

[44] García, *Mexican Americans*, p. 28.

[45] Pycior, "La Raza Organizes," p. 95.

[46] Ibid., pp. 126–127, 128, 130, 132, 134, 136; Acuña, *Occupied America*, p. 170.

[47] Cotera, *Diosa y Hembra*, p. 73; Pycior, "La Raza Organizes," pp. 76–81.

[48] Pycior, "La Raza Organizes," p. 76.

[49] Gamio, *The Mexican Immigrant*, pp. 136–137.

[50] Roberto R. Treviño, "*Prensa y Patria*: The Spanish Language Press and the Bicul-

turation of the Tejano Middle Class, 1920–1940," *Western Historical Quarterly*, XXII (November, 1991), 451–472.

[51] García, "La Frontera: The Border as Symbol and Reality," p. 198; García, *Rise of the Mexican American Middle Class*, p. 35.

[52] Treviño, *"Prensa y Patria,"* p. 454.

[53] García, "The Mexican American Mind," p. 69.

CHAPTER SIX

[1] Victor B. Nelson Cisneros, "La Clase Trabajadora en Tejas, 1920–1940," *Aztlán: International Journal of Chicano Studies Research*, VI (Summer, 1975), 240.

[2] David Montejano, *Anglos and Mexicans in the Making of Texas, 1836–1936* (Austin: University of Texas Press, 1987), pp. 103, 104, 109; Terry G. Jordan, "A Century and a Half of Ethnic Change in Texas, 1836–1986," *Southwestern Historical Quarterly* 89 (April, 1982), 398.

[3] Mario T. García, *Desert Immigrants: The Mexicans of El Paso, 1880–1920* (New Haven: Yale University Press, 1981), pp. 30–31; George Coalson, "The Development of Migrant Farm Labor System in Texas, 1900–1954," (San Francisco: R&E Research Associates, 1977), p. 2; Neil Foley, "Mexican Migrant and Tenant Labor in Central Texas Cotton Counties, 1880–1930: Social and Economic Transformation in a Multicultural Society," *Wooster Review*, No. 9 (Spring, 1989), 95–99.

[4] Montejano, *Anglos and Mexicans in the Making of Texas*, pp. 113, 149, 151.

[5] David Montejano, *Race, Labor Repression, and Capitalist Agriculture: Notes From South Texas, 1920–1930* (Berkeley: Institute for the Study of Social Change, 1977), pp. 11, 12; Montejano, *Anglos and Mexicans in the Making of Texas*, p. 173.

[6] Nelson Cisneros, "La Clase Trabajadora," pp. 241, 244.

[7] Montejano, *Anglos and Mexicans in the Making of Texas*, pp. 129–130, 143, 148, 253; Evan Anders, *Boss Rule in South Texas: The Progressive Era* (Austin: University of Texas Press, 1982), pp. 90–91.

[8] Richard A. García, *Rise of the Mexican American Middle Class, San Antonio, 1929–1941* (College Station: Texas A&M University Press, 1991), pp. 38–39; Arnoldo

De León, *Ethnicity in the Sunbelt: A History of Mexican Americans in Houston* (Houston: Mexican American Studies Program, 1989), pp. 11–12.

[9] Montejano, *Anglos and Mexicans in the Making of Texas*, pp. 114, 162–163, 168, 232.

[10] Ibid., pp. 191–192; Guadalupe San Miguel, Jr., *"Let All of Them Take Heed": Mexican Americans and the Campaign for Educational Equality in Texas, 1910–1981* (Austin: University of Texas Press, 1987), p. 24.

[11] Emilio Zamora, Jr., "Mexican Labor Activity in South Texas, 1900–1920" (Ph.D. Dissertation, University of Texas at Austin, 1983), pp. 42–43; Carole E. Christian, "Joining the American Mainstream: Texas' Mexican Americans During World War I," *Southwestern Historical Quarterly*, XCIII (April, 1989).

[12] De León, *Ethnicity in the Sunbelt*, p. 25.

[13] Jovita González, "America Invades the Border Towns," *Southwest Review* XV (Summer, 1930), 476–477.

[14] Manuel Peña, *The Texas Mexican Conjunto: History of a Working-Class Music* (Austin: University of Texas Press, 1985), p. 116.

[15] García, *Desert Immigrants*, pp. 211, 213–214, 217–219; Guadalupe San Miguel, Jr., "Social and Educational Influences Shaping the Mexican American Mind," *Journal of Midwest History of Education Society*, XIV (1986) 58; De León, *Ethnicity in Sunbelt*, p. 13.

[16] García, *Desert Immigrants*, pp. 117–122; San Miguel, "Social and Educational Influences," pp. 58–59.

[17] San Miguel, *"Let All of Them Take Heed,"* pp. 25, 19.

[18] González, "America Invades the Border Towns," p. 477.

[19] Christian, "Joining the American Mainstream," pp. 559, 569, 577.

[20] Ibid., pp. 586, 574, 584.

[21] Ibid., pp. 582–583.

[22] Ibid., pp. 559–560.

[23] Zamora, "Mexican Labor Activity," pp. 112, 104–105.

[24] Ibid., pp. 223–224, 216, 179, 155–156, 157, 161, 181, 171–172.

25 Ibid., p. 186.
26 Ibid., p. 198; García, *Desert Immigrants*, p. 99.
27 García, *Desert Immigrants*, pp. 107–108.
28 Julie Leininger Pycior, "La Raza Organizes: Mexican American Life in San Antonio, 1915–1930, as Reflected in Mutualista Activities" (Ph.D. Dissertation, University of Notre Dame, 1979), pp. 137–138; Rodolfo F. Acuña, *Occupied America: A History of Chicanos* (3rd ed.; New York: Harper and Row, 1988), pp. 164–165, 170.
29 Zamora, "Mexican Labor Activity," pp. 200–201.
30 Carey McWilliams, *North From Mexico: The Spanish-Speaking People of the United States* (New York: Greenwood Press, 1968), p. 113; Mark Reisler, *By the Sweat of their Brow* (Westport, Ct.: Greenwood Press, 1976), p. 142.
31 Arnoldo De León, "Blowout 1910 Style: A Chicano School Boycott in West Texas," *Texana*, XII (1974).
32 Zamora, "Mexican Labor Activity," pp. 66–68; Montejano, *Anglos and Mexicans in the Making of Texas*, pp. 116–117; José A. Hernández, *Mutual Aid for Survival: The Case of the Mexican American* (Malabar, Florida: Robert E. Krieger Publishing Co., 1983), p. 72; Sylvia Alicia Gonzales, *Hispanic American Voluntary Associations* (Westport, Ct.: Greenwood Press, 1985), p. 120.
33 Anders, *Boss Rule in South Texas*, p. 220; Montejano, *Anglos and Mexicans in the Making of Texas*, p. 117; Don M. Coerver and Linda B. Hall, *Texas and the Mexican Revolution: A Study in State and National Border Policy* (San Antonio: Trinity University Press, 1984), pp. 85–108.
34 Montejano, *Anglos and Mexicans in the Making of Texas*, pp. 117–118, 125; Rodolfo Rocha, "The Influence of the Mexican Revolution on the Mexico-Texas Border, 1910–1916" (Ph.D. Dissertation, Texas Tech Univerity, 1981), Chapter 6; Coerver and Hall, *Texas and the Mexican Revolution*, pp. 85–108.
35 Edgar Shelton, *Political Conditions Among Texas Mexicans Along the Rio Grande* (San Francisco: R&E Research Associates,

1974), pp. 17–18, 34–36, 40–47, 60–66, 73–74, 74–76, 76–77, 79, 81–82, 84–86.
36 Lewis L. Gould, *Progressives and Prohibitionists: Texas Democrats in the Wilson Era* (Austin: University of Texas Press, 1973), p. 287; Montejano, *Anglos and Mexicans in the Making of Texas*, p. 292; Ignacio García, *United We Win: The Rise and Fall of the Raza Unida Party* (Tucson: MASRC, University of Arizona Press, 1989), p. 7.
37 García, *Rise of the Mexican American Middle Class*, p. 206; Shelton, "Political Conditions," pp. 74–76.
38 Anders, *Boss Rule in South Texas*, pp. 15, 266; Garcia, *Desert Immigrants*, pp. 170–171.
39 Anders, *Boss Rule in South Texas*, pp. 63, 221, 236, 192.
40 Ibid., pp. 152, 227, 246–247, 250, 266–273. Information on J. T. Canales made available to the author courtesy of the Texas State Historical Association, *Handbook of Texas*, revised edition (Austin: Texas State Historical Association, forthcoming); Frank L. Madla, "The Political Impact of Latin Americans and Negroes in Texas Politics" (M.A. Thesis, St. Mary's University, 1964), p. 72.
41 Christian, "Joining the American Mainstream," p. 594.
42 Douglas O. Weeks, "The Texas Mexican and the Politics of South Texas," *American Political Review* XXIV (August, 1930), 622.
43 Christian, "Joining the American Mainstream," p. 590, 589; Hernandez, *Mutual Aid for Survival*, p. 73.
44 Christian, "Joining the American Mainstream," pp. 589–590.
45 Ibid., pp. 589–591.
46 Roberto R. Treviño, "*Prensa y Patria*: The Spanish Langue Press and the Biculturation of the Tejano Middle Class, 1920–1940," *Western Historical Quarterly*, XXII (November, 1991), 461, 463–464.
CHAPTER SEVEN
1 R. Reynolds McKay, "Texas Mexican Repatriation During the Great Depression" (Ph.D. Dissertation, University of Oklahoma at Norman, 1982), pp. 101–107, 270; 566–571.

[2] Manuel Peña, *The Texas-Mexican Conjunto: History of a Working-Class Music* (Austin: Univerity of Texas Press, 1985), p. 126.

[3] David Montejano, *Anglos and Mexicans in the Making of Texas, 1836–1986* (Austin: University of Texas Press, 1987), pp. 168, 227, 232, 265.

[4] Ibid., p. 227; Pauline Kibbe, *Latin Americans in Texas* (Albuquerque: University of New Mexico Press, 1946), p. 125.

[5] Montejano, *Anglos and Mexicans in the Making of Texas*, pp. 174, 176.

[6] George O. Coalson, *The Development of the Migrant Farm Labor System in Texas, 1900–1954* (San Francisco: R&E Research Associates, 1977), pp. 23, 25.

[7] Carey McWilliams, *Ill Fares the Land* (Boston: Little, Brown and Co., 1942), p. 238.

[8] Ibid., pp. 238–239; Kibbe, *Latin Americans in Texas*, pp. 159, 177; Coalson, *The Development of the Migrant Farm Labor System*, p. 23.

[9] Richard A. García, *Rise of the Mexican American Middle Class: San Antonio, 1929–1941* (College Station: Texas A&M University Press, 1991), p. 39; Kibbe, *Latin Americans in Texas*, pp. 123, 126, 128; Arnoldo De León, *Ethnicity in the Sunbelt: A History of Mexican Americans in Houston* (Houston: Mexican American Studies Program, 1989), pp. 51–52.

[10] Peña, *The Texas Mexican Conjunto*, pp. 115, 127.

[11] Rodolfo F. Acuña, *Occupied America: A History of Chicanos* (3rd ed.; New York: Harper and Row, 1988), p. 240; De León, *Ethnicity in Sunbelt*, p. 62.

[12] García, *Rise of the Mexican American Middle Class*, p. 250.

[13] Nick Kanellos, *A History of Hispanic Theatre in the United States: Origins to 1940* (Austin: University of Texas Press, 1990), pp. 86, 100, 199; De León, *Ethnicity in Sunbelt*, p. 65.

[14] Mario Barrera, "The Historical Evolution of Chicano Ethnic Goals," *Sage Race Relations Abstracts* X (February, 1985), 6–7; Julie Leininger Pycior, "La Raza Organizes: Mexican American Life in San Antonio, 1915–1930, as Reflected in Mutualista Activites" (Ph.D. Dissertation, University of Notre Dame, 1979), p. 226.

[15] García, *Rise of the Mexican American Middle Class*, pp. 86–87.

[16] Roberto R. Treviño, "*Prensa y Patria*: The Spanish Language Press and the Biculturation of the Tejano Middle Class, 1920–1940," *The Western Historical Quarterly*, XXII (November, 1991), 463–471.

[17] Carole E. Christian, "Joining the American Mainstream: Texas' Mexican Americans During World War I," *Southwestern Historical Quarterly*, XCIII (April, 1989), 591–592; De León, *Ethnicity in the Sunbelt*, p. 80.

[18] García, *Rise of the Mexican American Middle Class*, p. 275.

[19] De León, *Ethnicity in the Sunbelt*, pp. 81, 86, 87–89; Montejano, *Anglos and Mexicans in the Making of Texas*, p. 232.

[20] García, *Rise of the Mexican American Middle Class*, pp. 301–302; Guadalupe San Miguel, Jr. "*Let All of Them Take Heed*": *Mexican Americans and the Campaign for Educational Equality in Texas, 1910–1981* (Austin: University of Texas Press, 1987), p. 76.

[21] Mario T. García, "Mexican Americans and the Politics of Citizenship," *New Mexico Historical Review*, LIX (April, 1984), 188, 198–199, 200–201.

[22] Everett Ross Clinchy, "Equality of Opportunity for Latin Americans in Texas," (Ph.D. Dissertation, Columbia University, 1954), pp. 188–189.

[23] García, *Rise of the Mexican American Middle Class*, p. 272; San Miguel, "*Let All of Them Take Heed*," p. 81.

[24] San Miguel, "*Let All of Them Take Heed*," pp. 85–86; Mario T. García, *Mexican Americans: Leadership, Ideology, and Identity, 1930–1960* (New Haven: Yale University Press, 1989), pp. 62, 72, 73.

[25] De León, *Ethnicity in the Sunbelt*, pp. 71–76; García, "Mexican Americans and the Politics of Citizenship, pp. 95–98.

[26] Juan Gómez-Quiñones, *Chicano Politics: Reality and Promise, 1940–1990* (Albuquer-

que: University of New Mexico Press, 1990), p. 48; Frank L. Madla, "The Political Impact of Latin Americans and Negroes in Texas Politics" (M.A. Thesis, St. Mary's University, 1964), p. 72.

[27] García, *Rise of the Mexican American Middle Class*, pp. 261, 266; Kibbe, *Latin Americans in Texas*, p. 220.

[28] García, *Rise of the Mexican American Middle Class*, pp. 261, 272, 281.

[29] Ibid., pp. 271–272; García, *Mexican Americans*, p. 42; De León, *Ethnicity in the Sunbelt*, p. 90; Benjamin Márquez, "The Politics of Race and Assimilation: The League of United Latin American Citizens, 1929–1940," *The Western Political Quarterly*, 42 (June, 1989), 360.

[30] García, *Mexican Americans*, pp. 38–40.

[31] Information on Alice Dickerson Montemayor made available to the author courtesy of the Texas State Historical Association, *Handbook of Texas*, revised edition (Austin: Texas State Historical Association, forthcoming).

[32] Acuña, *Occupied America*, p. 198; Victor B. Nelson Cisneros, "La Clase Trabajadora en Tejas, 1920–1940," *Aztlán: International Journal of Chicano Studies Research*, VI (Summer, 1975), 247.

[33] Arnoldo De León, "*Los Tasinques* and the Sheep Shearers' Union of North America: A Strike in West Texas, 1934," *West Texas Historical Association Yearbook*, LV (1979).

[34] Victor Nelson Cisneros, "UCAPAWA Organizing Activities in Texas, 1935–1950," *Aztlán: International Journal of Chicano Studies Research*, IX (Spring and Summer, 1978), pp. 73–74.

[35] Ibid., pp. 74, 75, 77.

[36] García, *Mexican Americans*, Chapter 7.

[37] Cisneros, "UCAPAWA," pp. 80–81; Kenneth P. Walker, "The Pecan Shellers of San Antonio and Mechanization," *Southwestern Historical Quarterly*, LXIX (July, 1965), pp. 44–58.

[38] Julia Kirk Blackwelder, *Women of the Depression* (College Station: Texas A&M University Press, 1984), p. 132.

[39] Acuña, *Occupied America*, pp. 223–224; Melissa Hield, "Union Minded: Women in Texas ILGWU, 1937–1950," in Richard Croxdale, *Women in the Texas Workforce Yesterday and Today* (Austin: People's History in Texas, Inc., 1979), pp. 8–11, 13.

[40] Blackwelder, *Women of the Depression*, p. 151.

[41] Montejano, *Anglos and Mexicans in the Making of Texas*, p. 269.

[42] Matt Meier and Feliciano Rivera, *Los Chicanos: A History of Mexican Americans* (New York: Hill and Wang, 1972), p. 186.

[43] Kibbe, *Latin Americans in Texas*, pp. 283–286.

CHAPTER EIGHT

[1] Terry G. Jordan, "A Century and A Half of Ethnic Change in Texas, 1836–1986," *Southwestern Historical Quarterly* 89 (April, 1986), 534–535.

[2] David Montejano, *Anglos and Mexicans in the Making of Texas, 1836–1900* (Austin: University of Texas Press, 1987), pp. 276, 286.

[3] Robert A. Calvert and Arnoldo De León, *The History of Texas* (Arlington Heights: Harlan Davidson, Inc., 1990), p. 348.

[4] Montejano, *Anglos and Mexicans in the Making of Texas*, pp. 263, 271–272; Calvert and De León, *The History of Texas*, p. 349.

[5] Leo Grebler, Joan W. Moore, and Ralph Guzman, *The Mexican American People: The Nation's Second Largest Minority* (New York: Free Press, 1970), p. 106; *U.S. Census of Population: 1960*. Final Report PC(2)-1B, "Persons of Spanish Surname," Table 1, p. 2.

[6] Guadalupe San Miguel, Jr. "*Let All of Them Take Heed*": *Mexican Americans and the Campaign for Educational Equality in Texas, 1910–1981* (Austin: University of Texas Press, 1987), p. 113; Montejano, *Anglos and Mexicans in the Making of Texas*, pp. 272, 273.

[7] Manuel Peña, *The Texas Mexican Conjunto: History of a Working-Class Music* (Austin: University of Texas Press, 1985), p. 128.

[8] *Dallas Morning News*, Dallas, Texas, September 13, 1987, pp. 22A–23A; Arnoldo De León, *Ethnicity in the Sunbelt: A History of Mexican Americans in Houston* (Houston: Mexican American Studies Program,

1989), p. 98; Rodolfo Acuña, *Occupied America: A History of Chicanos* (3rd ed.: New York: Harper and Row, 1988), p. 282; Oscar J. Martínez, *The Chicanos of El Paso: An Assessment of Progress* (El Paso: Texas Western Press, 1980), p. 6.

⁹Peña, *The Texas Mexican Conjunto*, pp. 128, 130; Carl Allsup, *The American G.I. Forum: Origins and Evolution* (Austin: Center for Mexican Americans Studies and the University of Texas Press, 1982), p. 21.

¹⁰Allsup, *The American G.I. Forum*, p. 21; Robert H. Talbert, *Spanish-Name People of the Southwest and West* (Fort Worth: Texas Christian University Press, 1955), p. 79.

¹¹Talbert, *Spanish-Name People in the Southwest and West* p. 62 (Table 28).

¹²George O. Coalson, *The Development of the Migrant Farm Labor System in Texas, 1900–1954* (San Francisco: R&E Research Associates, 1977), pp. 107, 115.

¹³Allsup, *The American G.I. Forum*, p. 21; Acuña, *Occupied America*, p. 276; Pauline Kibbe, *Latin Americans in Texas* (Albuquerque: University of New Mexico Press, 1946), pp. 174, 177, 179, 180–181.

¹⁴Peña, *The Texas Mexican Conjunto*, pp. 126–128, 130–131.

¹⁵Acuña, *Occupied America*, p. 277.

¹⁶Edward C. McConagh, *Ethnic Relations in the United States* (New York: Appleton-Century Crofts, 1953), pp. 194–195.

¹⁷Allsup, *The American G.I. Forum*, p. 104.

¹⁸George N. Green, "The ILGWU in Texas, 1930–1970," *Journal of Mexican American History*, I (Spring, 1971), 150–151.

¹⁹Acuña, *Occupied America*, pp. 277–278.

²⁰Montejano, *Anglos and Mexicans in the Making of Texas*, p. 270.

²¹Allsup, *The American G.I.Forum*, p. 25.

²²Montejano, *Anglos and Mexicans in the Making of Texas*, p. 270.

²³George N. Green, "The Good Neighbor Commission and Texas Mexicans," in Jerrell H. Shofner and Linda V. Ellsworth (eds.), *Ethnic Minorities in Gulf Coast Society* (Pensacola, Florida: Gulf Coast History and Humanities Conference, 1979), pp. 112–113, 124–125.

²⁴Allsup, *The American G.I. Forum*, p. 65; Ozzie Simmons, *Anglo-Americans and Mexican Americans in South Texas* (New York: Arno Press, 1974), pp. 296–315.

²⁵Montejano, *Anglos and Mexicans in the Making of Texas*, pp. 280–281; Ignacio García, *United We Win: The Rise and Fall of the Raza Unida Party* (Tucson: MASRC, University of Arizona Press, 1989), pp. 7–8.

²⁶Montejano, *Anglos and Mexicans in the Making of Texas*, p. 281; Matt Meier, *Mexican American Biographies* (New York: Greenwood Press, 1988), p. 217.

²⁷Frank L. Madla, "The Political Impact of Latin Americans and Negroes in Texas Politics" (M.A. thesis, St. Mary's University, 1964), pp. 73–74; James R. Soukup, et al., *Party and Factional Divisions in Texas* (Austin: University of Texas Press, 1964), pp. 133–134.

²⁸Mario T. García, *Mexican Americans: Leadership, Ideology, and Identity, 1930–1960* (New Haven: Yale University Press, 1989), pp. 74, 75–76, 77, 78, 79, 82–83; San Miguel, "*Let All of Them Take Heed*," p. 114; Montejano, *Anglos and Mexicans in the Making of Texas*, p. 279.

²⁹Sister Frances Jerome Woods, *Mexican Ethnic Leadership in San Antonio* (Washington D.C.: Catholic University of America Press, 1949), pp. 109–110; Eugene Rodríguez, *Henry B. González: A Political Profile* (New York: Arno Press, 1976), p. 47.

³⁰Allsup, *The American G.I.Forum*, pp. 33, 40–49; Montejano, *Anglos and Mexicans in the Making of Texas*, p. 279.

³¹De León, *Ethnicity in the Sunbelt*, p. 129; Henry A. J. Ramos, *A People Forgotten, A Dream Pursued: the History of the American G.I. Forum, 1948–1972* (Corpus Christi: American G.I. Forum of the United States, 1982), pp. 42–45.

³²San Miguel, "*Let All of Them Take Heed*," p. 117; Guadalupe San Miguel, Jr., "The Struggle Against Separate and Unequal Schools: Middle Class Mexican Americans in the Desegregation Campaign in Texas, 1929–1957," *History of Education Quarterly*, XXIII (Fall, 1983), 348.

³³Allsup, *The American G.I. Forum*, pp. 79–80.

[34] San Miguel, *"Let All of them Take Heed,"* pp. 118–119.

[35] Ibid., pp. 123–124.

[36] Ibid., pp. 125–126, 133–134; Jorge Rangel and Carlos Alcala, "Project Report: De Jure Segregation of Chicanos in Texas Schools," *Harvard Civil Rights-Civil Liberties Law Review*, VII (March, 1972), 326.

[37] San Miguel, *"Let All of Them Take Heed,"* pp. 142–143; De León, *Ethnicity in the Sunbelt*, pp. 135–136.

[38] Allsup, *The American G.I.Forum*, pp. 73–77.

[39] Ricardo Romo, "George I. Sanchez and the Civil Rights Movement,"*La Raza Law Journal*, I (1986), 342, 343, 353, 354, 357, 360, 361.

[40] Green, "The Good Neighbor Commission," p. 114; Clinchy, "Equality of Opportunity for Latin Americans," pp. 77, 87, 96; De León, *Ethnicity in the Sunbelt*, p. 132; Allsup, *G.I. Forum*, pp. 104–105.

[41] Allsup, *The American G.I. Forum*, pp. 103, 107–108.

[42] Ibid., pp. 109, 110.

[43] Félix D. Almaráz, Jr., "Carlos E. Castañeda, Mexican American Historian," *Pacific Historical Review*, XLII (August, 1973); García, *Mexican Americans*, p. 250; Félix Almaráz, "Carlos Castañeda and Our Catholic Heritage," *Social Science Journal*, XIII (April, 1976), 27.

[44] Mario T. García, *Desert Immigrants: The Mexicans of El Paso, 1880–1920* (New Haven: Yale University Press, 1981), pp. 287–288.

[45] Américo Paredes, *Humanidad: Essays in Honor of George I. Sánchez* (Los Angeles: Chicano Studies Center Publications, 1977), pp. 121–122.

[46] Marta P. Cotera, *Diosa Y Hembra: The History and Heritage of Chicanas in the United States* (Austin: Information Systems Development, 1976), pp. 82–84.

[47] "J. T. Canales," *Handbook of Texas.*

[48] Meier, *Mexican American Biographies*, pp. 174–175.

[49] Montejano, *Anglos and Mexicans in the Making of Texas*, p. 281.

[50] San Miguel, *"Let All of Them Take Heed,"* pp. 114–115; Montejano, *Anglos and Mexicans in the Making of Texas*, p. 280; Grebler, et. al., *The Mexican American People*, pp. 150–151.

[51] Montejano, *Anglos and Mexicans in the Making of Texas*, pp. 275–277.

CHAPTER NINE

[1] Robert A. Calvert and Arnoldo De León, *The History of Texas* (Arlington Heights: Harlan Davidson, Inc., 1990), pp. 399–400.

[2] Manuel Peña, *The Texas Mexican Conjunto: History of a Working-Class Music* (Austin: University of Texas Press, 1985), p. 131; and Mario Barrera, *Race and Class in the Southwest: A Theory of Racial Inequality* (Notre Dame: University of Notre Dame Press, 1979), p. 132.

[3] David Montejano, *Anglos and Mexicans in the Making of Texas, 1836–1986* (Austin: University of Texas Press, 1987), pp. 276–278; Calvert and De León, *A History of Texas*, pp. 385–387.

[4] Arnoldo De León, *Ethnicity in the Sunbelt: A History of Mexican Americans in Houston* (Houston: Mexican American Studies Program, 1989), p. 167.

[5] David R. Johnson, et al. (eds.), *Politics of San Antonio: Community, Progress, and Power* (Lincoln: University of Nebraska Press, 1983), p. 196. In 1961, President John F. Kennedy appointed Reynaldo Garza of Brownsville as the first Tejano Federal District Judge. Donald W. Whisenhunt, *Texas: A Sesquicentennial Celebration* (Austin: Eakin Press, 1984), p. 351.

[6] De León, *Ethnicity in the Sunbelt*, pp. 167–168.

[7] Ibid., pp. 168–169.

[8] Marilyn Rhinehart and Thomas H. Kreneck, "The Minimum Wage March of 1966: A Case Study in Mexican American Politics, Labor, and Identity," *The Houston Review*, XI (1989).

[9] Guadalupe San Miguel, Jr., *"Let All of Them Take Heed": Mexican Americans and the Campaign for Educational Equality in Texas, 1910–1981* (Austin: University of Texas Press, 1987), pp. 167–168.

[10] Rodolfo F. Acuña, *Occupied America: A History of Chicanos* (3rd ed.; New York: Harper and Row, 1988), p. 377.

[11] Ignacio García, *United We Win: The Rise and Fall of the Raza Unida Party* (Tucson: MASRC, University of Arizona Press, 1989), pp. 10–11; De León, *Ethnicity in the Sunbelt*, p. 174.

[12] San Miguel, *"Let All of Them Take Heed,"* pp. 169–177.

[13] Ibid., pp. 177–181. Guadalupe San Miguel, Jr., "Mexican American Organizations and the Changing Politics of School Desegregation in Texas, 1945–1980," *Social Science Quarterly*, 63 (December, 1982), 710.

[14] San Miguel, *"Let All of Them Take Heed,"* pp. 192–194, 195–196.

[15] García, *United We Win*, pp. 11, 17; Carlos Muñoz, *Youth, Identity, Power: The Chicano Movement* (New York: Verso, 1989), p. 51.

[16] De León, *Ethnicity in the Sunbelt*, pp. 175, 176, 177.

[17] García, *United We Win*, pp. 24–26, 29.

[18] Ibid., pp. 37, 41; John Staples Shockley, *Chicano Revolt in a Texas Town* (Notre Dame: University of Notre Dame Press, 1974), pp. 120–124.

[19] García, *United We Win*, pp. 29, 45, 46–47, 49; Shockley, *Chicano Revolt*, pp. 127–138.

[20] García, *United We Win*, pp. 47, 50; Shockley, *Chicano Revolt*, pp. 133, 181–183.

[21] García, *United We Win*, pp. 19, 20, 50, 53, 56–57; Muñoz, *Youth, Identity, Power*, p. 101.

[22] García, *United We Win*, pp. 59–60, 62–63; Shockley, *Chicano Revolt*, pp. 183–189.

[23] García, *United We Win*, pp. 72–73.

[24] Ibid, pp. 84, 128.

[25] Ibid., pp. 61–62, 152, 156, 157–161, 164–165, 166–168.

[26] Marta Cotera, *Diosa y Hembra: The History and Heritage of Chicanas in the United States* (Austin: Information Systems Development, 1976), pp. 107–108; García, *United We Win*, p. 230. Information on Maria L. de Hernandez made available to the author courtesy of the Texas State Historical Association, *Handbook of Texas*, revised edition, (Austin: Texas State Historical Association, forthcoming).

[27] García, *United We Win*, pp. 33, 229–230.

[28] De León, *Ethnicity in the Sunbelt*, pp. 196–198.

[29] García, *United We Win*, pp. 180–181, 189, 190, 191, 205–206.

[30] Ibid., pp. 208–209, 210, 213; Montejano, *Anglos and Mexicans in the Making of Texas*, p. 289.

[31] García, *United We Win*, pp. 202, 227, 219.

[32] Montejano, *Anglos and Mexicans in the Making of Texas*, pp. 289, 290–292; De León, *Ethnicity in the Sunbelt*, p. 198.

[33] García, *United We Win*, pp. 231, 229.

[34] Laurie Coyle, Gail Hershatter, and Emily Honig, "Women at Farrah: An Unfinished Story," in Magdalena Mora and Adelaida R. del Castillo (eds.), *Mexican Women in the United States: Struggles Past and Present* (Los Angeles: Chicano Studies Research Center, 1980), pp. 117–144.

[35] *Nuestro*, November 1979, p. 25; *Texas Observer*, Austin, Texas, February 3, 1978. p. 10.

[36] *Nuestro*, January 1979, pp. 27–28.

[37] *Texas Observer*, April 17, 1981, pp. 4–5.

CHAPTER TEN

[1] *Census of Population, 1990*, Summary Population and Housing Characteristics (Texas), Table 3, p. 69.

[2] *Census of Population, 1980*, Detailed Population Characteristics, Texas, PC80-1-D45, Table 194, p. 45–8; *Census of Population, 1980*, General Social and Economic Characteristics, Texas, PC80-1-C45, Table 59, p. 45–59.

[3] *Newsweek*, June 8, 1987, pp. 27–28; San Angelo *Standard-Times*, San Angelo, Texas, December 16, 1989, p. 12A; December 17, 1989, p. 1A.

[4] David Montejano, *Anglos and Mexicans in the Making of Texas* (Austin: University of Texas Press, 1987), pp. 299, 285; Rodolfo F. Acuña, *Occupied America: A History of Chicanos* (3rd ed.; New York: Harper and Row, 1988), pp. 378, 379.

[5] Carlos Muñoz, *Youth, Identity, Power: The Chicano Movement* (New York: Verso, 1989), pp. 175, 184.

[6] Acuña, *Occupied America*, pp. 379–380.

[7] Montejano, *Anglos and Mexicans in the*

Making of Texas, p. 287; Muñoz, *Youth, Identity, Power*, pp. 175, 176.

[8] Acuña, *Occupied America*, p. 382; Muñoz, *Youth, Identity, Power*, pp. 178, 181.

[9] Muñoz, *Youth, Identity, Power*, p. 175; Acuña, *Occupied America*, p. 421.

[10] Arnoldo De León, *Ethnicity in the Sunbelt: A History of Mexican Americans in Houston* (Houston: Mexican American Studies Program, 1989), pp. 203.

[11] *Texas Almanac, 1976–1977*, pp. 612–613, 566–571, 572–579; *Texas Almanac, 1990–1991*, pp. 378–380, 384–398.

[12] Montejano, *Anglos and Mexicans in the Making of Texas*, pp. 293, 294.

[13] Ibid., p. 291.

[14] Acuña, *Occupied America*, p. 418; Juan Gómez-Quiñones, *Chicano Politics: Reality and Promise, 1940–1990* (Albuquerque: University of New Mexico Press, 1990), p. 195.

[15] Acuña, *Occupied America*, p. 378; De León, *Ethnicity in the Sunbelt*, p. 206.

[16] Acuña, *Occupied America*, p. 417; *Texas Observer*, July 29, 1988, p. 6.

[17] Matt Meier, *Mexican American Biographies* (New York: Greenwood Press, 1988), pp. 245–246; Sylvia Alicia Gonzales, *Hispanic American Voluntary Organizations* (Westport, Ct: Greenwood Press, 1985), pp. 157–160.

[18] Guadalupe San Miguel, Jr. *"Let All of Them Take Heed": Mexican Americans and the Campaign for Educational Equality in Texas, 1910–1981* (Austin: University of Texas Press, 1987), pp. 185–186.

[19] Ibid., pp. 197, 198–200.

[20] Ibid., pp. 201, 208, 209, 210.

[21] Ibid., pp. 173–174.

[22] San Angelo *Standard Times*, October 3, 1989, p. 1A, 5A; June 7, 1990, p. 1.

[23] *Texas Observer*, April 17, 1981. p. 5.

[24] Ibid., February 2, 1979, pp. 18, 19; April 17, 1981, p. 6.

[25] Letter of Rebecca Flores Harrington to author, December 19, 1990, in author's files.

[26] *Texas Observer*, April 17, 1981, pp. 6, 7; September 11, 1981, p. 8; May 17, 1985, pp. 6–7.

[27] Letter of Rebecca Flores Harrington to author, December 19, 1990, in author's files; *Texas Observer*, May 17, 1985, p. 7.

[28] *Texas Observer*, March 21, 1986, p. 11.

[29] Montejano, *Anglos and Mexicans in the Making of Texas*, pp. 306–307; Muñoz, *Youth, Identity, Power*, p. 182.

[30] Montejano, *Anglos and Mexicans in the Making of Texas*, pp. 299–300; David R. Johnson, et al. (eds.), *Politics of San Antonio: Community, Progress, and Power* (Lincoln: University of Nebraska Press, 1983), Chapter 9; Roberto E. Villarreal, "EPISO and Political Empowerment: Organizational Politics in a Border City," *Journal of Borderlands Studies*, III (Fall, 1988), 85.

[31] De León, *Ethnicity in the Sunbelt*, pp. 214, 215.

[32] Terry G. Jordan, "A Century and A Half of Ethnic Change in Texas, 1836–1986," *Southwestern Historical Quarterly* 89 (April, 1986), 395, 298.

Index

169

A native of Robstown, Texas, Professor De León received his undergraduate education at Angelo State University. Upon graduation in 1970 with a B.A. in history, he went on to Texas Christian University, where he received his M.A. (1971) and his Ph.D. (1974) in history.

Since then Professor De León has published widely in the field of Mexican-American history, though he specializes in the history of Texas Mexicans. His major works include *The Tejano Community, 1836–1900* (1982), *They Called Them Greasers: Anglo Attitudes Toward Mexicans in Texas, 1821–1900* (1983), *Ethnicity in the Sunbelt: A History of Mexican Americans in Houston, Texas* (1989), and *Tejanos and the Numbers Game: A Socio-Historical Interpretation from the Federal Censuses, 1850–1900,* which he coauthored with Kenneth L. Stewart in 1989. *The History of Texas,* which he coauthored with Robert A. Calvert in 1990 for Harlan Davidson, Inc., is used in many Texas colleges and universities.

Professor De León teaches in the Department of History at Angelo State University, where he holds the C. J. "Red" Davidson Professorship in history.

Mexican Americans in Texas: A Brief History was developed, copy-edited and proofread by Andrew J. Davidson. Lucy Herz was production editor. Graphic Composition, Inc., typeset the text, and the book was printed and bound by McNaughton & Gunn, Inc.

Cover design by DePinto Graphic Design.